AAW-1357
VC- Grad Studies

P9-CDK-491

Becoming Somebody:
Toward a Social Psychology of
School

lease remember that this is a library book,
and that it belongs only temporarily to each
person who uses it. Be considerate. Do
not write in this, or any, library book.

WITHDRAWN

In memory of my sister Helen and her
'gang', the Delilahs.

Becoming Somebody:
Toward a Social Psychology of School

WITHDRAWN

Philip Wexler

With the assistance of:
Warren Crichlow
June Kern
Rebecca Martusewicz

 The Falmer Press

(A member of the Taylor & Francis Group)
London • Washington, D.C.

UK   The Falmer Press, 4 John Street, London WC1N 2ET

USA The Falmer Press, Taylor & Francis Inc., 1900 Frost Road, Suite 101, Bristol, PA 19007

© P. Wexler 1992

All rights reserved. No part of this publication may be reproduced, stored in a retrieval system, or transmitted in any form or by any means, electronic, mechanical, photocopying, recording or otherwise, without permission in writing from the Publisher.

First published 1992
Reprinted 1996

Library of Congress Cataloging-in-Publication Data are available on request

A catalogue record for this book is available from the British Library

ISBN 0 75070 025 4 cased
ISBN 0 75070 026 2 paperback

Typeset in 11/13pt Times by
Graphicraft Typesetters Ltd, Hong Kong

Printed and bound in Great Britain by Biddles Ltd, Guildford and King's Lynn on paper which has a specified pH value on final paper manufacture of not less than 7.5 and is therefore 'acid-free'.

Table of Contents

Acknowledgments

I want to thank all the students, teachers and administrators in the schools in which we worked for several years for their cooperation, their patience, and especially for their interest. In the course of our research team discussions, there was interest from team members for a more 'action-research' orientation which would lead us to be involved in direct practices of educational change. Whether rightfully or not, this study is not a direct action-research work, although I do very much value this work that is being currently carried on by a number of my colleagues.

While I wrote the study, many people worked on the research of the study. I especially listed Warren Crichlow, June Kern and Rebecca Martusewicz because each one of them spent a good deal of time in one of the three schools in the study. In addition to Warren, June and Becky, Elaine Dannefer played an important research role. Also, Jeff Lashbrook, Todd Minkin, and Sharon Waldow assisted in the research. They are occasionally referred to as speakers in the text. As I indicate in the first chapter, the research was sponsored in part by the Office of Naval Research, but also by the Spencer Foundation and the University of Rochester. I am grateful to the administration and the faculty and students of the University of Rochester who have been supportive of many of my efforts during recent years. Margaret Zaccone and Jacqueline Sweeney assumed a major burden for the careful word processing of this manuscript.

I want to thank Doug Noble for his conversations about this and much other work. I want to especially thank Catherine Casey who worked as a graduate assistant with me for several years. Catherine worked on the journal, *Sociology of Education*, helped to coordinate *Critical Theory Now* (Falmer Press, 1991), and worked carefully on the editing and bibliographical work for *Becoming Somebody*. She has been a valued colleague as well as a highly capable graduate assistant.

I want to thank also my long time friend and colleague William F. Pinar for his supportive voice. Thanks also to Ivor Goodson for his ready colleagueship and his encouragement for my efforts in this manuscript. I want to thank Malcolm Clarkson, the Managing Director of Falmer Press, who with his acerbic wit and the sarcasm that he generously bestows, has been unfailingly supportive of my efforts in writing and in editing.

I want to thank my wife, Ilene Wexler for being who she is and also my children, Michael, Ari and Helen. I thank them for their love, understanding and tolerance. I hope that they will find this book readier to hand and easier to read than what we call the 'red and green books'.

Chapter 1

Horizon

Composition

In the long run, the reassertion of industrial capitalism and its culture may erase an emerging postmodern awareness in the postindustrial era. But, for now, there are deep cracks in the iron culture.

Recognizing the newer society of informationalism means rejecting the earlier industrial logic of mechanism and mirroring. In science, the backlash of an industrial culture has not yet succeeded in submerging the newer claims to describe what we know as being an artifact of human representation rather than an object espied through a non-refractory lens. To dismiss the information society's constructed way of knowing with the label of 'relativism' is an historically misplaced rejection of a movement that is post-structural and post-modern. It does not require taking leave of our senses and standards to acknowledge that in this culture, the old science of the social is finished in theory, if not in practice.

An interpretive, hermeneutic understanding of social reality does not mean abandoning the possibility of a real story, a comprehensible narrative, where there is care and attention not only to the form of telling, but also to the facts and to the characters of the story. But it does mean a deflation of pretenses, a modesty that leads to accepting the tenuousness of recognizable events and characters, and having a critical sympathy for the narrator's ineluctable involvement in her/his social humanity. Accounts of social life are composed during a time in history, in the life of the composer, and in a particular social world of resources and values. Perhaps great social analytic compositions transcend such contextual definition to offer timeless and placeless truths. On the other side of the coin, work that is entirely a reflection on the conditions and attitudes of social composition is not a satisfactory substitute for the composition itself. As Richard Bernstein (1983) put it, we want to go 'beyond objectivism and relativism'. Postmodern desire is ambivalent; we bask and glow in the light of our rejection of enlightened choices among certain alternatives. We love the out of bounds choice: neither/nor.

What that means here and now is that I offer my understanding of social life in three high schools as a structured narrative. The participants speak and I record and selectively re-present their voices. But to pretend that this is simply a dialogical construction of the facts of the case would be arrogant, exploitative and deceptive. I hear their voices in my ears, and I speak my words, conditioned by my place in historical social movement and by the language and analytical resources available to me.

Hopefully, I compose my account with an open mind and a revisionary attitude, abetted by a good set of records and transcripts and a well-tuned memory. But I 'take license'. I select, condense, juxtapose, underline, and, worst of all, I recontextualize lived worlds into an analytical social language. Still, I am not the cold-blooded instrument of an error-free objective knowledge-machine that mirrors social reality; but, an historical, social analytic composer, and what follows is neither Truth nor Fiction, but a composition.

Analytical Fields

I undertook a study of high schools as a retake of my first empirical effort, which was a participant observation study of a secondary residential school in Israel. In the time that elapsed between that research and this, field research or 'ethnography' of schools became popular among academic workers in education and later, in sociology of education (Anderson, 1989).

This 'new' sociology of education research was very tightly framed within prevailing models of social reproduction and resistance. Liberal faith in the reformative power of schooling, while partly displaced into a revived 'critical pedagogy', was generally eclipsed. The new sociology idea was that schools had the effect of more or less successfully replicating a stratified social order; notwithstanding instances of student cultural resistance against the socially reproductive structure of education.

I began these high school studies at that time in the early 1980s when there was incipient dissent from the reproduction/resistance model among the educationists and sociologists who comprised new sociology of education. The dissent, however, was in very much of an abstract and often polemical register. I was a dissenter, arguing for a social movement and symbolic interest rather than for the emphasis on the correspondence of school and workplace or on social and cultural reproduction and student resistance that was popular among the new sociologists of education. It was not until the end of the decade, in the field research of Lesko (1988), Weis (1990) and Crichlow (1991), that the dissenting view was expressed in case studies.

These high school studies express a mixture of the search for a less 'mechanical' and more symbolic view of social relations and for a more dynamic, movement rather than reproductive orientation to society. Yet, the connection between work and school that Bowles and Gintis (1976) had so powerfully and influentially expressed and the ideas of reproduction and resistance popularized by Apple, (1982), Giroux (1983) and Willis (1977) are also carried along in the way that I frame these accounts of social life in high school. The ghosts of Lukacs' (1971) structured totality and Althusser's (1969) relatively autonomous apparatuses vie with Touraine's (1981) societal self-production and Levi-Strauss' (1963) deep symbolic structure as stage setting beneath the limited and provincial abstract arguments and debates among a small group of new sociologists. But, I did undertake, perform and write the studies within and against the analytical field of the new sociology of education.

I rebounded from the academic purges of the late seventies in a private university in a corporate town. It was a good time for corporatism generally and, later, especially for corporatism in education. My research on high schools was first written for the Office of Naval Research, and funded as grant number N0014-83-K-0032. Like Bowles and Gintis (1976), military and corporate investigators were interested in the correspondence between schooling and working. The 'Best Years' research project was formally titled, 'Learning Commitment and Disaffection in Educational Organizations' and promised to explain the social relations of educational disaffection as the organizational socialization prologue to disaffection in the workplace.

While I was no less critical of corporatism than of new sociology of education, the high school studies were conceived with a military and corporate consumer in mind. The research was supported by a military-corporate-university establishment that was at least as serious as new sociology in its desire to explain education as a social process. The critics argued that schools succeeded too well and the establishment complained that schools were failing to perform their socially-allocated functional responsibilities. I brought both views into the field

3

research, a social class cultural 'carrier', in Weber's (1963) sense, for the skeptical wing of the corporate professional new middle class.

New sociology in academic theory and corporatism in educational practice are immediate contexts for the conception, performance and writing of this field research. The wider social, cultural and intellectual atmospheric circles are no less various and contradictory. The thinking and writing of social research in education takes place not at some clear intersection of historical social trajectories. More accurately, our work is now pervaded with interlacing synthetic strands of language and meaning that belong to different formations that vary not only in their basic directions and interests, but also in the times of their origin and moments of vitality. 'Archaeology' is not an accidental term for the layered formations of intellectual work during these times. Nor is 'postmodernism' an esoteric description of architecture or dance or even literature that occurs far from the scene of doing academic social science.

Postmodern images of eclecticism and pastiche that denote mixtures and combinations of style and intent also characterize expressions that are much closer to the legitimate and sustaining core of the culture. But legitimation demands a better front, and so we write social and cultural studies as if there were a clear analytical bridge between an unambigous object of vision and a mechanical procedurally correct or purely conceptually ideal seer. The discomforting alternative is to recognize that the multiplicity and simultaneity of channels, media and messages characterizing postmodern culture is also the condition of social research.

The older rhetorical forms of univocal competing hypotheses can still be invoked, but can be maintained only through shutting down a few broadcasting networks or turning up the sound/image volume so high that simultaneous messages are denied. Polyvocality is not a theory for precious literary analyses; it is the historical condition of our work. Only systematic suppression and denial saves us from confronting the fact that we live now not only beyond objectivism and relativism, but also beyond subject and object.

At the same time that the wider ambient social formation moved deeper into global corporatism, there was a mini-renaissance of academic social theory. The corporatist tendency, even when considered separately, has been complex. At the cultural level, free market beliefs and restorationist organicism coexist as the New Right agenda of the Reagan-Bush era. Institutionally, the corporatist social structure which melds state, corporation, and labor elites into horizontal ruling groups across sectors, solidifies beneath the cover of an asocial, individualist ideology of non-intervention.

Education was an excellent example of this synchronic cultural-institutional movement. Choice, voluntarism, and professionalism were spoken while horizontal integration of state school management, teacher union labor leadership, and private corporation executives openly pressed for a common program of educational 'restructuring'. This corporatism is the emergent institutional infrastructure that goes beyond the reassertion of capital and polarizing immiseration of labor to create a new society to manage the technology of informationalism. It is a reorganization of the economy, the polity, and the practices within which the postmodern culture of fractionated image, electronic icon, and technology-as-science is produced.

The academic mini-renaissance of social theory seemed to occur ideationally, as if there were no social organization of cultural creation, no polity, no economy. Self-centeredness was the explicit theme of this 'renaissance' as well as its unconscious practice. The auto-referentiality of language or irreducibility of the text were the cultural complements of self-centered meditations on the decentering and disappearance of the self. Social deracination permitted, however, attention to internal structures of symbolic meaning and to the signifier as independent of a strict representational correspondence to objects and persons. Foregrounding the symbolic domain took the wind out of the sails of simple realism and empiricism. A new holism, even though it prophesied dispersion, appeared in descriptions of discursive 'epistemes.' Philosophical anti-foundationalism still raised foundational questions about knowledge and social theory. The articulation of postmodern culture in university specializations created a common academic language of literary, symbolic, rhetorical and interpretive interests. Even sociology admitted postmodern theory along with hermeneutics and semiotics (Turner, 1990).

Such is the contradictory field of events, practices and analytics in which the composition occurs: new sociology and corporatism; symbolic theory and correspondence between school and work; social class polarization and the horizontal integration of different sectors. Geertz (1980) began the decade with the announcement that the style of discourse in social studies was becoming one of 'blurred genres'.

I think it is less a matter of blurring than of a synthetic interweaving of social and cultural history into the language of social analysis. The refraction of our lens is an historical translation of structures, formations and events into languages of frames, orientations and theories. Social history is recounted by a creative intervention that can only be made from culturally accessible materials. Ethnography is neither an objective realist nor subjective imaginative account. Rather, it is an historical artifact that is mediated by elaborated distancing of culturally embedded and internally contradictory (but seemingly independent and coherent) concepts that take on a life of their own as 'theory'. So, this is not 'news from nowhere', but a theoretically structured story where both the story and its structure are part of my times, and perhaps also of yours.

Theory

A truly postmodern story is simultaneously an exposition and a deconstruction of itself. The theoretical structure of this field research did not formally and expressly precede the research; nor did it emerge as a fitting conclusion to the data collection. Rather, the observations and the interviews nourished some preconceptions and let others atrophy. The theory is really a 'fusion of horizons' between the elements of the analytical fields as I blended them and what the subjects of the study said and did. I let the subjects lead me to the language and understandings that could only be found on the field of perception for which I had prepared.

That field is social interaction. The public preoccupation with school dropouts and the more esoteric critical theory inquiry into the motivational deficits of individuals as an aspect of the historic societal crisis of legitimation are expressions of a long-standing sociological interest: to understand the individual-society relation generally and, particularly to explain how and why people give their loyalty and energy to a social regime. The terms commitment and disaffection could be replaced by others like solidarity and alienation or integration and differentiation. On the surface, the question comes from Durkheim, but also from Marx, Weber, Nietzsche, Sartre and beyond.

The new sociology formulation of reproduction and resistance was, despite its Marxist trappings, too Durkheimian, too cultural, and finally, even too cognitivist for my interest. The social interactionist tradition of the American Pragmatists answers the individual-society relational question by showing how the individual is socially constituted, how society is in the individual. The structuralist critique, whether Marxist or Durkheimian (classical or modern linguistic and symbolic versions) is that the interactionists' view of society is diffusely organicist and does not represent the determined, organized, structured character of the societal pattern. I came prepared with a strong structuralist predisposition, but also the sense that historical events (and not simply theoretical discoveries and debates) had made it impossible to think of social structures or forms of culture as solid and stable entities.

The effect of a structuralism that is wary of solidity and reification in theories as much as in everyday life is to find the patterns of movement that are internal to and constituent of, any object, concept or system and then to reconstruct them. When I tried to encapsulate what students were doing in these high schools, their words summed it up best: becoming somebody. They were not struggling to become nobody, some high postmodernist definition of a decentered self. They wanted to be somebody, a real and presentable self, and one anchored in the verifying eyes of the friends whom they came to school to meet. The ideology of individualism that had such a successful comeback in North America during the first, Reagan phase of corporatism, and the anti-self self-centeredness of postmodern criticism oddly combined to underline again for me sociology's long-standing quest to subvert the bourgeois individualism of modern culture. Subcultural explanations only displaced the internal social dynamics of the self to a higher realm of 'culture.' Becoming somebody was an organizationally patterned process of production that used cultural resources deeply ingrained in more pervasive societal structures of inequality and difference.

The familiar language of social control was no more a clue to dynamic processes of movement internal to the organizations than was the term subculture for understanding patterned individual differences. Instead, the organization set the terms for a system of interchanges in which the 'somebody', self or identity was the valued product. I came to see a person's self or identity in these settings as a subjective value. This value was not entirely the product of the organizational field, because kids came to school with histories of value and with different repertoires of social and cultural resources that they could use to create the value of the subject, self or identity. But, within the intense social life of the school organization, some personal resources were ignored, while others were seized upon, used and affirmed as collectively valuable — building up in the process their possessors' image of identity. Identity was the pay-off for deposit of organizationally usable interactional resources. The flow of these resources, their transformation and use was not in a chaotic field, but was structured by the collective self-image of the organization and its distribution of values. In each school, I found an organizational economy of identity, that refuted both the restorationist ideology of individualism and the postmodern ideology of self-dissolution.

The organizational economy of identity was not an autonomous self-regulating system of social interactional resource interchanges. I chose the schools because I saw differences among public schools as aspects of differences among social segments more generally. I set out to see how the dynamics of commitment and disaffection might be different in socially disparate schools. This can be called a 'class' orientation in the sense that I do not take the superficial term 'school' or even 'public school' as an erasure of the very deep differences and inequalities that make this a highly stratified society; ideologies of individualism notwithstanding. I was not prepared, however, to discover *how* deeply the differences of class run in the lives of high school students. There are other differences that powerfully organize different experiences of everyday life, notably gender differences, but also age, racial, ethnic and regional differences.

I argue that class difference is the overriding organizing code of social life that sets one school apart from another. Against the background of a seemingly shared mass youth culture, what students struggle for in becoming somebody and how they engage that interactional life project during high school — the 'best years' of their lives — is different depending on where their school is located in the larger societal pattern of organized social differences and inequalities. The ideal and the route to becoming somebody in the *suburban white working class* is not the same as becoming somebody in a high school in a *professional middle class suburb*. Both are as different from *urban under class* among youths, as it is for their parents. Differences of achievement scores across schools are as well documented as differences in income among ecologically segregated communities of adults. What I underline is how much the experience and the meaning of everyday life — perhaps both cause and effect of achievement and income inequalities — are different. It is not simply a question of deficits or deprivations and advantages, but of different lifeworlds and of the dynamic organizational economies that generate and sustain diverse understandings and aspirations.

In portraying each school, I don't want to provide a snapshot of subcultures, under the sign of esotericism and voyeurism in which field research ordinarily flourishes. Rather, I aim to show an organized production process of subjective value. The 'product' of this process is identity, selfhood, the 'somebody' which the students work to attain through their interactions in school. The process is the organized shaping of a distribution of images of identity. These images may not capture the full reflexive biographical psychodynamics of a person's self, but they make a difference for how the student defines herself and is reciprocally defined by and defining of friends, teachers and parents. These images of self are stereotypes, relatively unrefined, almost caricatured types of social identities. But, students and teachers work with them and produce them in the course of their interactions.

The social process in the organization is the way that single behaviors, words, or other kinds of signs become representative of the self. There is a structure of social or identity 'tracks' in the schools, and while there are cross-overs and some people who are neither within one imagic, tracked world nor another, for most the identity image production process consists of amplification, distortion, condensation, representation and diffusion of partial signs that denote full identities. Smoking does not make you a 'drugger' or a 'radical', but smoking in the druggers hall or 'on the rock' might well put you on a track that goes through an official set of identity confirming organizational practices.

These practices are highly structured, dividing within class and gender into identity types which are the 'somebody' that you have become. This self-realization is not of course ordinarily a case of mistaken identity, but culminates a build up of suitable signifying repertoires of language, speech and action that qualify for a typification of identity. The organization is an economy because it sets up standards or values and social instruments to achieve them, moving and shaping identities and the interactional resources used in their accomplishment. 'Getting detention' is not only an organizational sanction that restricts student movement, but a message from the social instrument of the discipline structure that shapes a more general image of who you are in the context of school life. 'Good kids' get detention, but 'burn outs' and 'scum' are processed, defined and recycled within the detention punishment structure. Likewise, 'elites' and 'stars' are created in the gymnasium and its corridors, the school literary magazine or in official student councils.

These identities are not random or pluralistically tolerant and inclusive. In each school, types of selves are set by the central image of the school and the organizational devices used to achieve its image, whether of 'school spirit' or 'bright students' or college 'prep'. These images are social class emblems. They stand for important aspects of life for the social segment in which the school is located. Within each class image that sets the values implemented by organizational structures like dean's offices, departments, alternative programs, and pupils' social and psychological services, there is an internal stratifi-

cation, a binary division between those students who will become —
according to the social class and organizational emblem — winners
and those who will be losers. There is an internal class polarization of
students because the identity tracks are hierarchically arranged and
divided between good and evil.

Each student contributes to his own self-production by the
interactional labor that he performs. Paul Willis (1977) was right to
say that students unintentionally, even in their resistance to school
life, contribute to social reproduction. But their contribution is not
simple class affirmation. It is not their opposition which is the important
fact, but the work they do in performing it. New sociology replicated
the Manichean good and evil organizational worlds of schools in the
terms of good resistance and evil reproduction. In the class structured
organizational lifeworld, students are systematically engaged in the
symbolic interactional labor through which they become somebody.
While students are aware of the educational afterlife in the occupational
work world, and in varying degrees acknowledge interest in attention
to the learning of school subjects, I find that their central and defining
activity in school is to perform the social interactional labor which
enables them to establish at least the image of an identity. In turn, that
image, I think, then further organizes the course of their lives. The
primary tracking in school is of the self, and students are not victims
but symbolic workers in the identity production process. 'Losers' are
both self and organizationally produced. 'Dropping out' or 'pushing
out' is the withdrawal of student labor, although less evident forms of
production sabotage and slow downs occur in schools.

For each of these schools, I try to describe the structured processes of interaction, the symbolic labor and interchanges through which
a limited number of stereotypical and stratified identity images are
produced.

I would like educators to draw the implication of how serious are
the limitations on the current movement for what I would call 'cognitive reform'. Even decentralized restructuring of schools and empowerment of teachers misses the point that the main thing about
schools is that they are one of a very few remaining public interactional
spaces in which people are still engaged with each other in the reciprocal, though organizationally patterned, labor of producing meaning
— indeed, the core meaning of self identity.

The general critical social theory questions raised first by
Horkheimer (1972) and in our times by Habermas (1982) about the
personally consequential meanings of a societal systems crisis in legitimacy and, in later industrial capitalism, of the administrative colon-

ization of the lifeworld are concretely enacted in the socially divided class worlds of students' social experiences. Against that background, postmodern and postindustrial informational and communicational paradigms are also being exemplified in the symbolic labor of adolescents. Within a mass electronic image production apparatus, which may well be the future universal process of self-production, people are still working at identity production — however crude and stereotypical — through interactional labor with others in concrete local organizations like schools. The importance of school interaction in identity-formation may itself be ideological, as the utopian or dystopian promise of the electronic village arrives to supplant face to face interaction as a creative historical force. For now, however rearguard, becoming somebody is action in the public sphere. What I hope to show also, for the socially interested reader, is that school experience is a small slice of a bigger and richer story of what social class life is like in a stratified American society. What follows is a chapter on each of three high schools within the same metropolitan area. Together with the research team, which at one time included eight people, I spent almost three years on and off in these schools. We conducted structured interviews with more than three hundred students, teachers and parents. Not all of our research, which later included a quantitative analysis of questionnaires, nor all of the schools in the original study are presented or analyzed here.

In the next three chapters, the theory is 'embedded' in what I call the descriptive analysis. In the remaining chapters, the embedded theory is articulated in a more general way, but can, I believe, be well referenced back to the earlier chapters as well as to our extensive library of transcripts. The theoretical chapters are an effort to give some empirical and social meaning to current discussions of post-modernism in culture and society. Beyond that, I try to make a beginning to an empirical historical analysis that was alluded to in an earlier book *Critical Social Psychology*, *(1983)*. I hope that this sets the stage for a next, larger study of social interaction, class and character in American society.

Chapter 2

Working Class: Nobody Cares

The architects who design American high schools must have a keen ecological sense; they do not all look alike. Grummitt High School is on a main road out of town, past the shopping malls, but not yet in the farm country. It is nested between the tract housing developments that you see off the road and the one level brick small industrial parks, like those that landscape the highways leading in and out of most American cities. Grummitt High School looks like one of these small industrial parks, with their adjacent car parking lots, which sometimes give the appearance of being public buildings by flying the American flag out front.

On approach, you can see clusters of youths not only at the drive-up front entrance, but in pockets of the building's inner perimeter, exitways that are not flush with the outer wall, but enclosed within brick cave-like exits. These are called the 'alcoves'. 'Visitors are welcome', states the sign past the front door. 'You must check in at the office', reads the next line.

> I have heard a lot of kids say that this place is a prison. I was out in the courtyard there, sort of in front of the school talking to people and someone was saying that it was a penitentiary, and it almost felt like that. You know those yards in a penitentiary where little groups cluster and hang around, where they have time they go out and then they have to be brought back in? A lot of kids joke about it and laugh because they see the parallel so clearly it is almost ironic.

I spent two years hanging out part-time at Grummitt. The last time I was back, after a few months hiatus, I was reminded that the feeling of hallway life was different than the usual brisk movement of between class changes in high schools. There is a tenseness, an aura of emotional containment, of suppressed violence. Yet, Grummitt is not an especially violent place. Despite claims that among the eight hundred students more than a hundred knives could be found on any day, there are only a few violent incidents, isolated grudge fights between friends and rivals. It is not the violence which sets the surface tone and coloring of the interactive, 'social feel' of the place. It is the containment.

Apparatus

During the early 1980s, when we did our field study at Grummitt High School, American society was already officially into a 'restorationist' social regime. The restorationist cultural agenda was, and still is now, to restore respect for authority and to resuscitate the moral authority of traditional institutions. For educational institutions, opinion polls showed that parents considered lack of discipline as the number one problem in schools. The restoration was a reaction against the torn social fabric of the Vietnam era, but more deeply against the liberal humanism that was seen as responsible for the permissiveness *malaise*, cultural decadence and social disorder resulting from the decline of traditional institutional moral authority.

Grummitt parents generally agreed, and they were happy that a change was taking place at their high school.

> I'll tell you one thing. Ten years ago you didn't say the word 'discipline' at any school meeting. Honestly. It got so that I'd sit there and I'd think: 'Something's wrong here.' Because literally, you didn't say that word. And now we're back to saying discipline again, and knowing that it's an expectation.

Teachers and administrators remember a time, only a few years ago, when at Grummitt 'permissiveness and humanism were going haywire'. There were stink bombs in the halls, kids fighting all the time, milling around and lateness. There was 'chaos'. The school was 'out of control'. Then, at the beginning of the 1980s, discipline began to be restored. The administrative apparatus for discipline that was considered ineffective was disbanded and one office was established with the disciplinary charge. There was, as a teacher who lived through those times noted, 'a tremendous change'.

13

'Somebody has to be the policeman', says the assistant principal for discipline. 'Somebody has to enforce the rules. There are teachers who cannot. There are teachers who find it very difficult to do it; someone has to do it. They might be very good in the classroom. They might be a very good educator. They might teach very well, but when they get themselves in a discipline situation they cannot do it.'

The school's disciplinary figure has both a rational accounting scheme and an ideology. Students who break a rule are 'written up', either by one of the hall monitors, also known as aides, a teacher, or an administrator. Being 'written up' means getting a 'referral'. The student is referred to the discipline office. A referred or written up student can either go directly to the discipline office center, be escorted there by an aide or teacher, or, most often, 'called out' of class, either by telephone or discipline office staff, to report to the discipline chief. In an average day, two hundred referrals might be written. Referrals are, however, only the first step. In the discipline office, students discuss their rule infraction with the administrator for discipline, assistant principal Mr. Bech. Some may receive reprimands and warnings, while others, on the average of forty a day, receive 'detention'. Detention means sitting in an empty designated room after school for as little as one school period or as much as an entire day, 'all day detention', so called.

Mr. Bech's ideology represents a sympathetic attempt to understand the wider context that generates rule-breaking actions and leads to the recidivist types whom he, and other teachers and students, call 'the losers'.

'They aren't into the education theme', the assistant principal begins, 'Plus the country itself produces fewer people that are going to be of benefit to the society as a whole. The 'me generation' — you have more people from that generation on welfare in that seven or eight year span than any other age group, and that will continue right on. And you still have the flower children walking around who are now wearing three piece suits. They still have that basic philosophy. A lot of them have surrendered that, but they really can't cope and they still fantasize. When they deal with their kids and when you deal with them, you find a lot of them are frankly out to lunch'.

'Now among the teachers', he continues, 'their parents had money and kids really didn't have to work that hard for their education, and I think they began to have this "me genera-tion". Everything had been given to them. If you looked at what happened to a lot of those people who then went into education you find they are the arch conservatives. But if you put them in an intellectual frame they still hold those ideals, and *it is a constant fight between us* because they look for order and control in their classrooms, but in talking with kids, they are still spouting the ideologies of the sixties.'

'As for the parents', Bech continues, exploring the contradic-tions, 'Many of them will sit home and voice these anti-estab-lishment whatever. Yet they don't expect the kid to do that because they don't look at themselves as the establishment, as part of the authority. But they exercise that authority, and expect the kid to adhere to that authority, and the kid gets confused. The kid brings it into schools, and the brighter kids will learn how to cope with it. It is the kids who aren't too swift who have the problems of adjusting because there is an awful lot of pressure on them from the peer groups and the problem of cutting classes — that is the way they show their rebellion. If somebody wants me there, I won't go.'

Becky: Is that the attitude?

Mr. Bech: A lot of times. And at other times I can't figure out why they cut classes. *I have never been able to figure out why a kid would cut.*

The restoration, like Mr. Bech, has both a 'rational accounting' and an ideological aspect. Its 'rational' program was, and still is, dismantling and elimination of the state welfare apparatus of the earlier 'permissive' and 'chaotic' liberal regime. In the educational sector, that meant reduction of funding for a variety of compensatory education programs. Locally, at Grummitt, the welfare retrenchment manifested itself by a severe reduction of an alternative program for students that focused on interpersonal counseling and the building of students' self-esteem. The youth workers in the program headed by Dr. Lyborg were going to be dismissed, and the entire program was slated for extinction.

Dr. Lyborg was someone, students said, who would 'listen to you. She treats you like a person, not like a prisoner'. The HELP program had its own large room, at the far end of a corridor on the opposite of the building from the discipline office. Students met their youth workers and counselors there, participated in self-clarifying and self-esteem group work session led by Dr. Lyborg. She did not like Mr. Bech, or the atmosphere of discipline in the 'new order'. 'These students need counseling, even 'heavy duty' counseling', Dr. Lyborg said. 'Many of them have had harsh family experiences. They are vulnerable and we need to help them gain a sense of security. I don't know what they will do if the HELP program is closed'.

A newcomer to the school compared the HELP program with the discipline office in the following way:

> I've been sort of noticing that there is a split here in this school. I don't know if this is accurate or not. On the one hand, there's the real disciplinary crackdown, authoritative force. On the other hand, there's a group of people who seem to be more concerned about students' needs, concerned about asking questions about why kids aren't motivated, instead of cracking down on them for lack of motivation.

One of the students in the HELP program wrote a letter to the school district superintendent. Aside from the name changes, this is the letter which the student wrote:

> My name is Jack Fremen. I am writing to you about the fact that I am in HELP, and I was just informed that HELP is going to be cut from the school district budget. While I feel that this is a big big mistake, and the fact that there will be no more youth workers makes me even more mad. I feel that you should reconsider that fact and keep some of the workers. If it weren't for the workers many of the kids would have dropped out, and I feel that I would have to go without someone to talk to on a one-to-one basis. I also believe that Dr. Lyborg can't handle 80 to 100 kids on a one-to-one basis.
> Thank you.
> Jack Fremen

The restoration was a call for a 'back to basics', not only for traditional morality and institutional authority, but also in the forms of social knowledge. The 'cutbacks' meant a decline in support for the extra-curricular. The 'basic' subjects were not those that empha- sized the aesthetic dimension. At Grummitt, while theater was considered important alongside sports, resources for theater were re- duced. The main theater coach, Mrs. Fairbanks, was going to quit because she felt that her efforts were unrewarded. 'There just isn't enough support for extra-curricular participatory activities. . . . There are so many hassles. . . . The only rewards come from working with the kids themselves'.

'Kids live in the moment', says Mr. Bech, 'so you have to find something that makes them immediately uncomfortable. I used to try to get them to stop cutting classes by making believe that I was upset with them: "Hey", I would say, "you cut my class and I'm ticked off with you", You know, I'd put it on a personal basis. But if that doesn't work, how can I force them to class? Well, I can force them by giving them detention'.

The 'new order' pacified the halls and diminished open and organized student peer group opposition to the administration, but it did not eliminate class cutting or 'skipping'. It created a public grid for selecting and processing students in the disciplinary apparatus, for branding and, at the end point, extruding 'the losers' from the public school. These are the students who are already clustered at the perimeter of the apparatus, gathering to smoke or 'party' in the inner and outer alcoves of the building. These 'alcovians' or 'rads' as they are known ('I think', one student hypothesized that, 'the name came from the 1960s or something, when there were people who opposed things and were called radicals'.) while no longer in violent opposition to the school are in continuous friction with the apparatus of discipline.

According to the 'rads', 'Things have gotten stricter. When I first got here, there were one or two monitors in the hall, usually teachers. Now they are crawling all over the place, and still the kids that are there to get out of the halls they don't listen to them anyway, and I think half of them are afraid of the kids anyway'.

'Well, I mean you can't walk two feet without getting hassled. I walk down these hallways and get stopped every six feet by seventeen different hall monitors. We figure just this morning they busted about eighteen people in the alcove'.

Student: There is like no freedom in this school.
Becky: What kind of freedom?
Student: Like wherever you go you are always hassled. They are always asking you for passes and stuff like that. Also, there's no place to go out here. You have to come to school to see your friends.

Getting 'nipped' and 'written up' for skipping classes or smoking in the inner alcoves is the first stage of the disciplinary process. The second stage is an encounter in Bech's disciplinary office, where punishment is determined. One of the 'rads' describes the experience:

Well they send someone down from Mr. Bech's office to wherever you are, and then they just tell you to get your books and go down to Bech's, and you sit there for like an hour, biting your nails off because you don't know what you did. They try to use intimidation, but a lot of people just see through it, and they don't care anymore because they have been down there so much.

Student:	I was just very resigned, I waited there and I just sat back. I knew that I was going to go up there and say I don't care, give me detention. That was my whole attitude. I don't care because I know I won't go. If he gives me all-day fine — I won't yell and scream.
Philip:	What happened then? You sat and you chewed your nails for an hour, and then what happened?
Student:	Mr. Bech walked in, and he goes — there were thirty people in there, and he just takes his time — walks in and looks around, and he takes out these little sheets that have referrals on then and calls your name and asks why you skipped or where you were or something like that.
Second Student:	You get a referral or something, and he won't give you a chance to explain, or when he does, he won't believe it. If you try to explain he won't give you a chance, and when he does . . .

For 'rads', encounters with the disciplinary apparatus is condemnatory and escalating. 'Bech makes you feel like you're an inmate at Attica. He thinks that punishing people is going to straighten them out. Some of the people, they don't care if they get a referral or not. Punishment isn't going to stop them'.
The escalation of the vicious circle is described:

Student:	Well, I cut study hall one time.
Todd:	And they put you in all-day (detention) for that?
Student:	Well it built up to that. I got caught cutting study hall, and he told me, he says: 'To make up for it you

can sit two days in half a period of detention' —
that's my lunch period, fifth period. He said: 'Half
fourth period you sit in detention two days in a row,
then you'll be done'. I went to one half fourth period, the next day I just forgot about it. He called
me down two days later and says: 'Now you gotta sit
in sixth, seventh and eighth period'.... Instead of
being at work, I had to wait two periods, so I could
go to detention. I went to one of those, and then he
called me down and gave me all of these detentions
that I had to go to, or be suspended.

Second Student: But it goes up. Like first you might get after school
detention, then, if you keep doing it, you might get
all day. Then, if you keep doing that, you get suspended.

Third Student: And I don't see what good it does for me to go sit
in a damn room all day. Three days in a row, not
getting any of my work done ... I've been suspended
four times since October, for not going to eighth
period study hall, smoking halfway in and halfway
out of the alcove, and supposedly, I told one of the
aides to fuck off and die, which I didn't, which is
because I told Mr. Bech where he could shove it.

Fourth Student: All-day detention is like jail, you know. It's beat.
You get two passes — one in the morning, one in
the afternoon. You can go out for five minutes, you
know, to the ...

Fifth Student: I never listen to that five minute baloney.

A voice from the other side of the fence, Bech:

If the referral is written for cutting a study hall or something
like that its one thing, but if it is cutting an academic class then
it has a lot more consequences ... If they cut an academic class
they usually get detention, depending on what year they are in.

As I said, it is the immediate consequence. They don't show up
there a couple of times, and then they end up in all-day. That
is even worse, so you take away the frivolous cutting that builds
up the habit of cutting, that turns it away from being frivolous.

The original Bech plan was to call only in the mornings. I don't have the staff in the office. We are running about ten percent above last year. I think that you understand that if I call about three hundred, it is impossible not to break up a lot of classes. I am only calling now on Monday, Tuesday and Thursday, but it means that the turn around time is slower . . . I understand. You get the phone call and dump five kids out of your class. It is disruptive. There is no other way to pull them out of class. There is no other way — unless we do it in large lots.

Bech is not alone in running the disciplinary apparatus. The principal, Dr. Joe Kingman led the effort to restore order and control to Grummitt. He is an outgoing man, and is well-liked by many students and teachers. Others see him as a self-centered leader who thinks that 'Joe Kingman IS Grummitt High School'. His disciplinary style is more direct and personal than Bech's; not a part of the rational accounting of the disciplinary apparatus. One of the field research team provided this observational account of the more personal disciplinary style:

A teacher came into the office and said 'Isn't something going to be done about this kid out in the hall mouthing off'. Kingman stormed out and confronted the student. He was leaning over the kid with his hands on his hip and shaking his finger, and in a very loud voice telling him that he wasn't going to be allowed, and to get his butt in the chair. The kid sat down, and when he mildly tried to protest, Kingman screamed even louder and leaned over the chair and told him that he has threatened the last teacher that he was ever going to threaten on this faculty . . . I thought he was screaming and ranting and raving like a lunatic, but nobody else seemed too surprised or particularly embarrassed. They were totally nonchalant. Two minutes later everybody moved over to where the faculty meeting was, and it was like the incident had never occurred.

Rads, Jocks and Thespians

The rads believe that they are caught in the vicious circle of a disciplinary apparatus that defines their relation to the school. At the same time, they see the apparatus operating selectively, so that it is not the behavior that is being punished, but the person doing the behavior. The apparatus is unfair, but indelible. It stamps your image, and however much you hate the school, you need an image to have friends and self-confidence.

Everybody needs an image. It tells you where to be in the morning, before first period class, what to wear, who to hang out with, what to think and feel — especially about school and other kids. You have to work to become somebody; otherwise you become a 'grug', a nobody with no place, no alcove, no gym or library entranceway to hang out in and to meet your friends — your friends who confirm who you are. The rads, the jocks — the athletes and just plain ordinary 'Joe and Jane Grummitts' or 'good kids' — and the thespians, who seek recognition to parallel the jocks (even wearing sport type school jackets, signifying theater) although the jocks disdain them, all are doing the work of becoming somebody. Even the favored jocks and good kids work at having an image. I was told even 'being a student leader is hard work'.

The rads do a lot of this work through mass cultural identification. They wear heavy boots or wooden spike high heel shoes. They wear leather jackets or tee shirts with hard rock group insignias. When they hear the word 'Harley', they associate directly and recontextualize it to the motorcycle emblem, Harley Davidson. But, they are also doing some of their image work, the becoming somebody, in their collaboration with the disciplinary apparatus.

The disciplinary apparatus is escalating and selective.

Student: Its a vicious circle, 'cause once the kids start bumming out on the teachers or the curriculum, or whatever, then they skip classes, or whatever, and then they have to come down harder on them, which makes the kids hate them more, which makes them come down harder and harder and pretty soon it gets out of control. And that's why two hundred people a day get called down for referral.

Rads tell two stories. Vicious circle is one and the other is selective punishment. The 'vicious circle' is confirmation of negative or 'rad identity' by the apparatus:

It's not that we can't handle the responsibility or the rules or anything, it's — if we break the rules just once, it's like *branded on us*, that we broke the rules, so if there's a rule broken and we just happen to be around, it's us who did it, nobody else.

21

And no matter what we say or do, you know, will change it.
Unless our parents help out.

In rad folklore, parents are not likely to fare much better in their
encounters with the apparatus. This lore offers a variety of explanations for the initial rule infraction — 'for one reason or another . . .
there's a million things'. But, to the students what matters is the image
branding.

When I first got here, it was scary. I used to sit with Irene who
was one of my old jock friends, because I was confused. I
never knew what I could do with myself because I never labeled
myself. I got labeled and I decided 'OK, if they want to label
me I will just find out who is worth being friends with and I am
not going to care'.

But students do care about their image. 'For three years now, I
realize that I've worried about putting up a front, trying to outdo the
image'. The image gets set early: 'Well, a person gets a fixed idea
about them and then everybody thinks the same way'. The image-
making is conjoint and interwoven, between the apparatus and peers.
Selective punishment is the channel that fuses the two methods of
image making. Some jocks or 'good kids' and rads are known to the
hall monitors and get by or get 'nipped' according to who they are.
But selective response may depend on the image itself. Clothing is the
clearest signal. A 'good kid' recounts how she negotiates the hallways
safe from 'write ups' or referrals, without the required pass:

Student: Like now I don't even use passes at all. Going to the library
today I just happened to get one. If I have time; I do, but
usually I don't.

Philip: Well, aren't you worried about getting caught?

Student: No. They never stop me. If they ask me I say no, I don't
have a pass. Some of the aides in the hall get mad. But
usually they go 'OK' and I keep walking.

Philip: Do you think that they let everybody go like that or that
they know you?

Student: No. There's people that they stop all of the time.

Philip: So how do they know who to really stop do you think?

Student: I think it has a lot to do with the way you dress because I
dress up a lot and they don't seem to stop me, but the
people who wear jeans and tee shirts — they always stop
them. It is a stereotype, you know, but . . .

The public identification confirms, to the point of creating, the difference. 'Rads smoke publically; jocks smoke privately'. For all the anguish it causes, you need to have an image.

They know by the way I dress. I wear boots to school, and some people look just like 'Oh my god'. And you wear sneakers, and the other group looks at you like 'What a jock.' No matter what you wear, how you act, or what you do, *you're still going to get called something*.

The image is constraining, takes work, and is not always salutary. The struggle for this image is thought to bring the reward of self confidence. The image is made apparently unwillingly in encounters with the apparatus and in association with peers. But its also made in self-constructive, even self-mythologizing work:

It's all talk. Its so funny. I heard about a couple of fights that never existed just to make people look good. People would go home, come in the next day and say, 'Hey, I beat up this girl last night' to make themselves look good. I just have to laugh about it so bad.

Jocks also do self-constructive and self-mythologizing image work.

Becky: Why wouldn't you wear a leather jacket?
Student: I don't know.
Becky: Yes you do.
Student: Yeah, I do. A friend of mine said 'I am going to buy a leather jacket for Christmas', and I thought 'No — you don't want to do that'. I just never thought about it. Because the people that I think of as doing that aren't the people I hang around with.
Becky: And why is that?
Student: Because *I have a set image*. I am not going to be a hypocrite. I think that too. I have met people before that aren't like that and they wear leather jackets. I know it's not true and I don't know why.

The image work of the apparatus, peers and self-construction are underlined by the smooth, packaging commercial work, not only of the mass media, external to the school, but to media packaging within the school. Here is an excerpt from a film used to sell high school yearbooks, a marketing device for the commercial outfit that sells the high school experience — repackaged — back to the Grummitt seniors. As they sit in the darkened assembly hall, the film begins with visual collage of protypical high school scenes. Against the audio background of popular music, the voice over for the presentation begins. The film is called, *The Best Years of Your Life*.

> Do these things look familiar? They should. They're the things you're doing right now, the things school life is made of. But will you be able to remember them ten or fifteen years from now? Today's the day you have to decide if you want to buy a yearbook. Don't make this decision lightly. Your yearbook is the most important purchase you'll make this year ... every year people call yearbook printers, trying to buy copies of their old year books ... Some of the people that call the printers looking for old yearbooks had a classmate who had become a celebrity. Take Farrah Fawcett Majors, for example. Do you think the kids in her class in Corpus Christi ever thought of her as a *Charlie's Angel*? ... *Each and everyone of you will be pictured in this year's annual. You will be imprinted, and we all know what pictures mean to us ...*

As Mr. Bech would say, there is a 'more immediate consequence' to image work; it brings self confidence: 'They gain self-confidence as they gain their own image. And they say, "well, that's my image, I must live up to it or I guess people expect it of me ..." You see it more when they're around other people ... they're trying to gain their image, gain their self-confidence'.

The image directs and encases appropriate behavior: 'Yeah. It would be cool for a radical to skip a class and go out and get stoned. But it wouldn't be cool for him right after school to go home and do all of his homework and come in the next day and be at every class. .... The jocks are afraid to lose control ... that would be uncool'. The ideal typical rad mold is for boys to be tough macho motorcycle and car buffs, and for girls to be sex objects. The boy appearance is longish hair, boots and leather vest with occasional flannel shirts and tee shirts with names on them, either hard rock music or motorcycle emblems. The rad girl also has an almost uniform appearance; jeans, short leather jackets, wood — spiked heeled shoes, and long coiffured hair, in the style of the *Charlie's Angel*, Farrah Fawcett Majors. Their relation with each alternates between living out the tough encasement or revealing needs for affection and dependency. The girls talk about dating and bar hopping with ambivalence.

Her? We go out with her, she's bad — she's big time. I mean she won't let me . . . She wanted to go home with Steve one night, first night she met him, alright? I said, 'You're not going'. She wouldn't give me my purse or get out of the car — well they were all drunk . . . Those two were fighting and screaming at each other.

The boys express the 'double-standard'.

Student: They don't act like girls. I wouldn't want a girlfriend like that.
Becky: What does a girl act like?
Student: Well, I want a girl that, a nice girl that doesn't talk dirty like that all the time, That's all they do, they don't act like girls. Don't you think so?
Becky: They are girls; it depends on your definition of . . .
Student: They don't act like ladies.
Becky: But you guys will sit around amongst each other and talk about your exploits, don't you?
Student: Not in front of girls, I wouldn't.

A woman teacher observes the rad girls 'dependency on male affection'. 'Okay, then they start to go with a guy, and it ends up that the guy abuses them, knocks them around . . .' In a momentary break from the macho mould, a rad boy talks about his need for affection:

My parents split up. They never hugged me once or anything like that. So what do I do when I get a girlfriend. The first thing I want to do is to get as close to her as I can. It is sort of like 'Be my girlfriend, my parent'.

Image work is disdained by a small group of rads: 'They put on an act and try to be something that they're not'. One offers a matter of fact job-like approach to school life, without consideration of 'getting an image'.

Student: I just take school as an everyday job. I mean, you put in your eight hours of work, you get it done, you pass. I mean, it's like you don't get paid. You receive no reward for it or anything else. But, the people in this school are ridiculous.

For many 'good kids', school is fun;

'You can do pretty much what you want here'.
'Students are happy; they like their teachers and their friends'.
'Grummitt is a good school'.
'I like all of my teachers'.

Good kids do, however, recognize image making as work. One of the leading jocks and all around 'Joe Grummitt' concludes his description of his activities in student life with the observation that: 'After you're eight years old, you don't have any fun'.

Participation in school activities leads to a change in image and self confidence — like other forms of relating to the apparatus. The sign of the organizational tie is different, positive rather than negative. But, the process of relation to the apparatus — altering images, reinforced by peer association, and leading to self definition, is very much the same. A student leader recalls her relation to sports and student activities of the school:

Student: When I was a freshman, I went to school and that was about it. You went to school, attended your classes and then you came home, whereas I have had a lot of changes in my life, through the leadership stuff . . . I thought 'God, why was I so stupid that I didn't get involved as a freshman . . .'

Becky: You were saying about the way you feel about yourself has a lot to do with getting involved here.

Student: Yeah, because the way I looked last year was a lot different than the way I look now because I have contacts and I got my hair cut.

Becky: Your hair was longer. Did you also get it permed?

Student: Yes I did. I have gone through a lot of changes over the summer and the last few years, and I think if I had to do this (being a student leader) last year I'm not sure I would feel as confident about it. I think that the friends that I have kept throughout the years are still my good friends. They still accept me for what I am, plus I have made more. It makes a big difference as how you see yourself, I see myself as better than last year so I think of myself as doing a better job.

Becky: You seem to feel pretty good about yourself, and the way I'm hearing you right now is that your participation in things here and your success has had a lot to do with the way you feel about yourself.

Student: Yeah. Plus the way the others view you too. It is amazing

26

that whenever I come in wearing a skirt, people say . . . *it is
all in the way you dress too . . .*

Good kids and jocks get the approval of school adults as well as
peers. 'Mr. Bech adores Ronnie Gates', students claim. Their feeling
in the school is not one of selective punishment, but of trust and
freedom of movement.

Student: We have more responsibility than when we were
freshmen, and we're getting more freedom. Like today, I had to get all this stuff ready. I went to the
librarian and said I need this cassette and projector
soon, and they said OK. They were very nice about
it, and I thought if it had been anybody else I wonder if they would have done the same thing. If they
would have trusted somebody like that . . . I didn't
have such a hassle — like go check with your teacher
or run around and get this person's signature, and
I thought 'Oh great'. This is just great. They were
so nice about it. . . . Sometimes it just works so
nicely . . . they know who you are. You know who
they are . . . Yeah, if you are willing to make the
effort, the teachers and students are willing to return it.

Second Student: You can also tell, at least if you are a student leader,
exactly where everyone is. In student meeting, you
know exactly where everyone sits. The right is always the black student union. In the middle you
have the well known jocks — the athletes, they are
upfront. Not that jocks are intelligent, but the intelligent people sit there. Then usually to the left there
are what is called the radicals — people who smoke
and cut classes.
The 'thespians' are the theater people. They represent the school, like the jocks, in collective events.
Their events are not the pep rallies where jocks and
cheerleaders 'crank up school spirit'. But they do
put on plays which are well attended by parents and
other adults in the community — representing the
good name of Grummitt to the collectivity and its
constituencies. Being a thespian has its advantages.

Student: I don't know, its just that we can get crazy *among ourselves*, you know and basically do anything we want.

Theater is a refuge for students who are not in the jock mainstream or in negative symbiosis with the disciplinary apparatus.

Student: I turned to theater because I really didn't know what else to do with myself really.

Becky: Was turning to theater really a fleeing?

Student: Yeah, at the time it was. I didn't know what it was going to be like, and I ended up getting a really good part that I really liked, and I worked hard at it and I became involved ...

Thespians are different: 'They wear bells on their shoes and tinsel in their hair ... carry around teddy bears. I guess that is them, but I wouldn't blame guys for not being attracted to that ...' The being different runs the risks of 'harrassment' in the halls. The jocks, who refer to radicals as 'scum', also denigrate thespians as 'faggots' and 'thespos'. Thespians stick together and even 'try to be inconspicuous' to avoid the 'put-downs' used in jock identity work. Lately, some students say, thespians have begun to assert themselves and to be proud of their identity. Still, they generally don't fight back. They are 'soft kids' — unlike the 'hard'-cased radicals.

At the same time, however, their coach fears further cutbacks, lack of resources and support, as part of the desiccation of participatory activities in the path of 'the basics'. Ideology and rationalization organize processes of group relations that on the surface appear as 'subcultures'. Thespians, even in their sensitive eccentricity, are also 'keeping up an image'.

Teachers see the student groups and image making process of becoming somebody. They see it from the vantage point of their own histories, and their own struggles for self confidence, inside the moving apparatus.

Teachers

The movement for teacher professionalism was already well underway by the early 1980s. But the sense of empowerment and hope for the future was, at least not yet, not evident among the mainstream of Grummitt High teachers. On the contrary, their historical sense was of decline, in their perception of teachers' social status in the community, their accounts of their daily work situation and its past and future trajectory, and in their sense of the students' values and capacities. What they describe is an historic moment of cutback and rationalization of teachers' work that unintentionally cuts out the central committed relation of mutual respect and caring between teacher and student. They describe how students see schooling and the pervasive 'not caring'. In doing so, they show also the erosion of the student teacher relation from the teachers' side; a teachers' not-caring that they want desparately to resist, but seem unable to overcome. They are disappointed that what they thought was social mobility became occupational stagnation, that what they thought was an irrepressible hunger for teaching was discouraged and stymied by their encounter with a rationalized administrative apparatus and students who did not feel at home in the school, and that what had been their calling was now reduced to a job.

Teachers began with optimism and a feeling of personal status mobility. Many entered their jobs during the 1960s, which they now see as a time of 'high morale' and progress in professionalism.

Teacher:

I come from a family which is primarily working-class people. . . . I come from an immigrant family. I was the first person in my family to graduate from high school. So there's a lot of personal, psychic reward for me being a teacher. . . . I came into the world of education feeling pretty good about the fact that I have succeeded. . . . So I don't feel that this is below me . . . Yet I find that there may be millions and millions of teachers out there who don't think that teachers are — you know, its no longer the honorable profession that it was.

Second Teacher:

I would like to think of myself as a professional, classified as a professional. Still, I wouldn't consider teaching a profession as far as when you compare with doctors as being a profession, or lawyers; in that context, it is not a profession.

When I came here in the mid-1960s, salaries were starting to get good. Then my friends, who when I started teaching thought 'Isn't it great that I was teaching. Poor slob, somebody has to do it. It is like you have got the calling. When the money got good, it was like because I had a nice car and a nice house, I was a bum, a leech on society. I really got the feeling — all of us did — that we were overpaid leeches on society with big vacations. Kind of like people were envious. Now it is swinging back the other way.

Third Teacher: In the 1960s we went through a period of, let's say, teachers finally realizing where they were, and what they were, and seeing other segments of the population fighting for higher pay, withdrawing their service and so forth. And we went through that as a district.

At the same time, however, by the end of the 1960s, cutbacks had begun. 'They took out the hatchet', as one teacher put it.

Teacher: Things that were proving themselves to be good and were getting reasonable results were cut. That is something else that goes on — as soon as anything works, the funding goes. . . . The foreign language programs disappeared. Writing labs were gone. Look at what's happening now with the HELP program.

The decline is the result of a combination of excessive control by the administration, insufficient resources for the 'extra' programs, a changing student population with more materialistic attitudes, and, above all, a non-caring. The result is routinization and burn out of teaching.

Teacher: You could probably relate this back to the budget cuts, you know, first big drastic ones — abolition of programs or to staff reductions and overcrowded high schools or lack of student interest. Maybe its the climate in America; we've never appreciated the pursuit of intellectuality.

The administrative control is described graphically as 'They'd step on your heels. If you try to fight something, they'd step on your heels. "It's my building", Kingman says. When he says, "I am Grummitt High", it's like Hitler saying, "I am Germany"'.

Teacher: I've had a lot of experiences where I've worked my ass off and I've felt — very frankly — that I was slapped in the face. . . .

Teacher: It's the bureaucracy that does it. It's the system. Try to have a standard, maintain and work it through a *system that could care less*.

The single most prevalent effect, according to teachers, is scaling down, pulling back, withdrawing into a ritualized job performance — 'burn out'. For the seasoned teacher, the process of retreat has taken place over many years, following the pullbacks from the 1960s. But now, new teachers can arrive at the same point quickly.

Teacher: That (ritualism) is not difficult. It takes two weeks of conditioning. Its like athletic training and it takes two weeks of conditioning. After two or three weeks of that you're in the groove. After vacations though, it's a little tough coming back.

Now, there is regulation, student materialism and lack of caring — from the administration, the system, and the students. Lack of caring is contagious. *The regimented attitude becomes instilled in about six months.*

Teacher: But those were the good old days, and it's no longer. If you're not really super-encouraged by your cohorts, you eventually learn to let it die . . . it's doing what everyone else needs to do, well not everyone, that's stereotyping. I would say the vast majority of people come in, they teach their class and they leave. . . . Very few people correct homework. I watch it. They check it off and throw it in the basket. I watch it day after day.

Second Teacher: Give yourself a couple of years and you will learn how to handle Grummitt. You will learn that *you do just what you are supposed to do, and nothing more and nothing less. And you will be a very happy person. So It isn't 'burn out'. It's just . . . do your job. Nobody cares.*

Third Teacher: So now, I don't get involved to that extent. Teachers just don't want to. Now, I do it just like the book states. And do you know what? As far as the administration is concerned, as far as the

	department chairman is concerned, as far as every-body is concerned, this is the best year I've ever had.
Philip:	How could I recognize burn out? What are the signs?
Third Teacher:	Yeah, I'm burned out right now.... Always tired, that's one. If you were at their homes, they probably don't sleep very well. They, well, just tend to be tired with the whole system. You know, they don't care.

The method of ritual adaptation becomes a norm: 'And I think you find that in any school you go to. The teachers that are really good and want the kids to learn something and really like to teach, are almost frowned on by others who just want to get by and lift themselves out of the position of being a teacher, and get into an administrative position'.

> Teachers split themselves between their school life and what they call their 'private life'.... A lot of these kids need more of the private — need more of the caring.

Other teachers defend against the criticism and self criticism of teachers. 'You know, there have been a lot of attacks on education from the world of business, that businessmen are accountable, and they're efficient and we're not. I worked in business and I worked in industry, and in many ways they're less efficient than we are.... Look at The Company. Everybody says if you could run schools like The Company, you wouldn't have these budget deficits and these problems with kids. And I pick up the papers and I see that Company employees are stealing, and taking long lunch hours. They could probably lay off 60 per cent of their workforce and keep up production'.

Professionalism is not being achieved at Grummitt High.

Teacher:	The way it is now, teaching objectives are submitted and they are approved by the administration. That approval cuts out professionalism. If I have to have an objective approved, that means that I'm not professional enough to take care of it.... Professionalism means self-direction.

Teachers' perceptions of students display the same sense of decline. Students no longer show them respect ('A kid can call you an s.o.b. and you've got to take it'.). The disciplinary apparatus has not provided the fuel for respect or altered the way of relating that turns teachers off from their students.

Teacher: I don't appreciate being wild. I don't appreciate not knowing how to come into a room — like some of the little things. Instead of knocking on a door when you want to come in, they will kick the door for no reason or they'll walk up and down the hall and every window gets pounded on. I mean to me that's anti-social. . . . and it continues . . . When I started out teaching, I couldn't spend enough time in the classroom. Kids used to always hang around. . . . *Now, all that's fizzled . . . students don't care anymore.*

Teachers complain about the 'little things', although one teacher describes differences of standards of cleanliness as 'class differences'. Generally, however, they despair of the materialism among students, which they see as a source of not-caring.

Teacher: Money, money. You hear a lot of talk about money . . . Yeah, most of what I get is a feeling of 'Well, I don't really need this anyway. I can go to work at The Company, on the assembly line. That's going to guarantee me a twenty thousand dollars a year right now and that can buy me a boat and a car. . . .' I had one instance where a kid — I said to him that I couldn't find any of his homework — he pulled out a pay check which was for a good sum of money, and he says, 'Here's my homework. This is my paycheck. What are you going to give me?'.

Teacher: The impression I get from most of the kids is that they expect, well maybe 90 per cent, to work over there (points out the window) at The Company. . . . You become companyized.
. . . They'll take any job for the bucks.

These are some of the explanations that teachers offer about why students 'don't care'. That the reasons for non-caring may be somehow deeply related to their own reluctantly induced non-caring is rarely mentioned. What they do know, is how much less they now care, and also, how much less their students care. These teachers have found various modes of adapting, but especially withdrawn their commitment from a 'system that doesn't care'.

Interaction

The conventional view that these are high school subcultures which organize action puts the cart before the horse. The subcultures and the individual identities which typify them are, in the first instance, the result of a system of social interaction. By that I mean more than that like-minded kids associate or even that the interaction between the students and the apparatus underlines some natural peer tendencies.

Instead, I suggest that all the types of collective identity that we see in the school are *compensatory reactions to an interactional relational lack*. The immediate cause of the rad identity, for example, is the combination of encounter with the disciplinary apparatus and its vicious circle of escalating social extrusion with mass culturally inspired peer models. The deeper cause is that formation of identity in relation to the apparatus — whether in Bech's office, Dr. Lyborg's HELP program, in thespian theater or in the athletic cranking of spirit by good kid jocks — is a derivative, compensatory mode of identity formation. These institutional methods, including the path of selective reinforcement and interactionally spiralling processes of image making, are substitutes for authentic committed relations in which identity is the result of more deeply rooted emotional commitment, comingling of selves, and caring. In other words, these are alienated methods of identity formation in which the interaction between the peers and the apparatus is a compensating substitute for shared creation of identity by ongoing and mutually contingent interaction. Instead, institutional methods — including even those such as HELP, which specializes in compensatory relating — have displaced the more organic and less institutionally rationalized spontaneous collective creation of identity or selfhood in social interaction. Indeed, the identities that we observe are what I would call 'reifications', abstractions that blot out their ongoing interactional basis so that we see only an end result rather than the process of collective creation. The reason for that in this case is that the authentic, organic interactional process has broken down, and has been replaced by an institutional or rationalized, even mechanical, alternative mode of self production.

Oftentimes, students and teachers recognize the interactional lack and derivative character of their relations. However, they attribute — rightly, in the sense of proximate or immediate cause — their selfhood to peers and apparatus. Of the replacement of relational by institutional means of self production, they can effectively signal only the lack, only a hint of what an unalienated mode of collective identity creation would be like. The pedagogic relation, the interaction between teacher and student, is the quintessential social relation. Yet, here there is a lack of the emotional commitment and caring that is required for the relation — teaching and learning — to be successful. Recognition by students and teachers of this lack, and of its displacement by apparatus defined abstractions of identity which the peer subcultural process then fills in what has already been 'rationally' outlined, is indicated by the simple phrase: 'nobody cares'.

This as a variant of Habermas' (1984) thesis of the dialectic of the rationalization of the lifeworld that precipitates crises of legitimation. The dessication of everyday socio-emotional life, the 'lifeworld', if you prefer, is multicausal and it comes at dialogical interaction from both sides. The reasons that teachers 'don't care' have to do in part with state-mandated rationalization of curriculum. But, they also have to do with the history and struggle of the movement for teacher professionalism and the retrenchment, rather than, as Habermas would have it, the extension of, the welfare state into everyday life. The disciplinary apparatus itself is second order, derivative or compensatory to liberalism's intervention in everyday life through such 'soft' institutional methods as the HELP program. It is a reaction to the failed 'permissiveness' of humanism. It is not liberal modernity, but the counterrevolution of the restoration which destroys the lifeworld and replaces it with reified caricatures of identity that social scientists mistakenly designate — compounding the reification — as natural subcultures that structure social interaction, rather than the reverse. Image making is alienated self production, during these times of the American Restoration.

'Nobody cares' is not only the result of cutbacks, inadequate professionalism and over rationalized administrative regulation on the teachers' side, and family neglect, mass media, poverty, materialism and general cultural 'backslide' on the students' side. The mutual non-caring — which comes from different sources on each side of the failed pedagogic relation — is a closed feedback loop. It is a reinforcing relation of failure and withdrawal. Students, as we shall see in a moment, say they don't care also because they believe (or at least some say that they do) that it is THEM — and not a self-protective ritual defense against the SYSTEM that doesn't care — who the teachers don't care about. And, of course, 'If they don't give a shit about me, why should I give a shit about them or about what they have to say'. My difference with Habermas is that rationality or undistorted communication is, in this instance, not firstly a matter of creating linguistic conditions for rational argument or ideal speech (although Habermasians, will claim of course, these social preconditions are just precisely what they mean). Regrettably, this hand tips to Durkheim, because what is at issue first and foremost is the sense of mutual commitment at an *emotional* level, of *caring* as the basis of relation. Grummitt High School, a 'working class' school, does 'repro-duce' the dynamic of alienated labor; but it occurs in the domain of selfhood and its images, and in a much more complex manner than neo-Marxist new sociologists could ever conceive.

Durkheimians, like Basil Bernstein (for an overview of his work see Bernstein, 1990), would be pleased that the educational crisis at Grummitt is a relational matter, and further, that there is a class difference of codes which seals the pact of absence, the non-caring mutual withdrawal. Teachers say, after all, that part of the problem is a class difference. The students don't know the 'little things', like knocking on a door before you enter a room; or they don't blow their noses, or are not clean enough, or are just generally, 'wild'. While a clash of elaborated and restricted class language codes exists, the meaning of codes has to be stretched. It is not a matter of cultural taste as code; 'They'd rather listen to Joe Schmo and his wackdown band'. Rather, as Bernstein understands it, is a behavioral code differ-ence in modes of relating, where the language difference is embedded and secondary to the relational action. It is 'a certain way with teachers' that the rads don't have, a 'way of handling themselves', that they indicate as the reason why jocks do better. It is the character of the interaction or mode of relation. However, while the relation is of course linguistic, it is premised and results in *emotional dynamics of identification, attachment and caring*. Where 'nobody cares', commu-nicative competence and linguistic similarity and/or difference is simply of no importance, even though the communication is an ingredient of the process of committed relation.

> And they try not to sound, you know ... that they care. 'I don't care' they keep saying, 'but that doesn't really bother me at all' and things like that, and you know and oh, it is just rippping them apart inside and it's horrible ...

There is a refrain of not caring, obviously more prevalent among the rads. But insitutional rather than relation identity formation even for the jocks and thespians presumes a personal relational distance in favor of the apparatus, even when it is of 'positive' valence, 'cranking up school spirit' through good kid athletics. The rads are negatively linked to the apparatus, and further out on the perimeter, it is easier for them to articulate the derivative process of identity relation that I call 'reified' or 'alienated'.

The teachers don't care you know, AND SO, neither do we.

The caring does work through communication, but less in linguistic code similarity and more in the emotional commitment dimension of relation that is signified by the other's willingness to listen. The willingness to listen, the 'paying attention' to me, and the inability to handle oneself effectively in the relation are the immediate and interwoven indicators of the non-caring relation.

Student: That is what we need more of. Instead of going and smashing and writing on the door or something, you should go tell someone your feelings.

Becky: Will the people listen if you tell them your feelings?

Student: That is the key . . . *if you can get someone to listen* when you talk, you have got the perfect system. But you can't . . . You need someone who really can make a difference . . . You look up to someone to find out if you did good or bad. Hey, did I do this good or bad? You are not going to look to someone your own age . . . And if you can't do that with someone, with an adult, then you are forced to do it with someone else. The only thing that they are going to compliment me on is vandalism, so naturally what am I going to do? *I have to get the attention* from vandalism.

A good teacher listens. He's fun. He listens. He says, 'Let's do this together'.

She would sit there and talk to you. She'd say 'Why don't you try this with me?'

The other side of listening and talking is 'gossip'; the interpersonal bridge to the apparatus that selectively reinforces identity labels without talking, and without caring.

'When you end up in Bech's, you haven't got a chance . . . You've got aides sitting there with their ear right next to Bech and its 'Dee dee dee o' one aide to the other. And they've got the whole gossip on you when you're here one day out of the whole year. It's gossip, gossip, gossip. They're talking about you or telling you what to do, and not doing it *with* you' — relationally.

Student: Everybody's always yelling at you: 'Grow up! Do this! Do that!'. And you're tryin' and everybody's always yellin' at

> you, and you're tryin' and not all of it's working out, and
> they'll get on your throat because it's not working out the
> way that they want it — they jump down your throat for
> that which — they don't have no right, because they push
> all this shit on us.

The jocks don't seem to have these problems — and they don't.
They are attached positively to the apparatus, but not primarily
to the direct interpersonally committed teacher/student relation; on
their side, the teachers are defending and adapting in ritual withdrawal
of relational commitment.

Student: For some reason, the jocks have got a way with teachers. If
             they need a pass for somewhere, fine. You can walk into a
             classroom behind a jock, and they'll say to me, 'Where's
             your pass?'. It always happens . . . It's like they don't want
             to help you.

The classes are 'boring'. 'Most of the students don't really care
because they find the class so boring they don't want to go. . . . You sit
there like a caged animal, listening to "Dee, dee". It's like the sound
of The Company'.
More importantly, the non-caring is active, and rad students feel
insulted and rejected — by the teachers who are offended and rejected
by them. 'There was this one teacher who was always saying, "Oh, you
are all losers". Yeah, and one day I came right out and asked him why
is he always picking on us? From then on, it was like, not a
problem . . . Teachers insulted three of the kids in our group . . . they
use cutdowns . . . But there is nothing you can do about authority.
Nothing. Authority doesn't want you to think. They just want you to
do . . .'
The effect is to bring to the surface the mutual non-caring, and to
explain student withdrawal on the ground of teacher withdrawal. 'No,
they don't care at all if you go to college. It's like they don't really
care one way or the other. You go or you don't go. Big deal. And this
is one of the major decisions of my life . . . They don't respect us,
we're not going to respect them . . . They think the kids are no good,
I guess that's it'.

> Now all that we can look forward to is getting high. Just to
> escape the reality that we can't control and won't be able to
> control. We could go bust our ass trying to be brilliant, you

know . . . The truth is, that is how many people feel. *I don't even give a shit what he thinks so it doesn't matter to me because I know that he don't care if I live or die.*

There are good teachers, the ones who listen and work with you. 'Yeah, they are the ones that try to teach you and the ones that really like their job. But the people who have been here for years, they don't give a shit anymore. They just want to get their money'.

The perception of materialistic instrumentalism that the teachers express about the students is reciprocated in the students' views of their teachers. 'Yeah, it's rare that you find a teacher that really takes the time and really enjoys being a teacher. You ask a teacher why do you teach, you know, and it's a job. I have to support my family. But not many of them would say that I enjoy teaching because I like helping kids'.

Some teachers are good. Some don't give a shit . . . I don't give a shit about them either . . . You just don't pay any attention to them. *If they don't care about you why the hell should you do what they want you to do?*

Teachers see parents as being primarily concerned with discipline: 'The parents who call me or the parents I have called, ask; "Well, is my kid behaving in class?" Well to me that means: Is he conforming to your rules? That's the most important thing — that's what they're concerned with the most is whether the kid is behaving'.

Even as teachers describe their own self-protective withdrawal, their ritual adaptation to a rationalized emptying of the committed pedagogic relation which they valued in their earliest teaching days, they indicate the need for caring relations as the basis for teaching.

Teacher: I don't know. I know that for them to learn, you provide comfort for them and they'll learn. You don't stuff things in front of them and expect them to learn. That's not how they learn.

Second Teacher: They want people talking to them. They want attention. I don't think that they're trying to be malicious when they do some of the things that they do. A lot of it is the attention.

Third Teacher: With our classroom situation we try to get numbers of bodies in a room and try to make it cheaper to educate them. There isn't the time to get to know them individually or time for them to learn to trust people, and as the education books all say number 1 is never to become emotionally involved, which means that you really don't care about your students. That is the big problem because they need someone to care.

Students describe the teachers who do care: 'They made the class real interesting. He was pretty crazy . . . he was more of a friend with students . . . You have to be on a friendly basis in order to be able to learn from someone'.

Without enough adult caring, kids turn to each other for support. 'What I see is almost *a hunger for social contact*'. The pedagogic relation flounders in the dynamic of mutual non-caring that occurs within the the school and the wider context of family and work life during the Restoration. The interactional principle governing the withdrawal of commitment is put best by a student; it is the 'likewise principle' — the rule of reciprocity as the over coding of a complex field of relations in which the pre-eminent, even caricatured, theme is 'nobody cares'.

Student: *So, it's likewise, you know. The teacher doesn't want to teach the kids who don't want to learn. Kids don't want to learn because they don't like the teacher.*

Chapter 3

Professional Middle Class:
Success Without Society

The End of Liberalism

When I came to Penbroke High in the early 1980s, the 'tightening up' that occurred five years ago at Grummitt had just begun. This 'tightening up' took place, however, against a different background, and it was implemented for different reasons — or at least with a different rhetoric. On a rare occasion, a teacher complained publicly about a 'general erosion of authority and discipline'. But that was not the usual tenor of the voices calling for change. The presenting problem, and simultaneously, its solution, was 'structure'. The most favored narrative of administrators and teachers was that the population of Penbroke suburb had changed and in addition, there were more family problems even among its customary denizens. As a result, students were unable to handle the 'freedom' and flexibility of the current social organization of the school; there was a need for 'more structure'.

The school prided itself on its flexible class scheduling system. By breaking the day into smaller time units that could be recombined to make short or longer classes, and not repeating the ordinary five day, eight period class organization, it had been successfully argued eight years before that more curricular electives could be introduced and that students would have more free or disposable time. Indeed, there were many highly specialized course offerings at Penbroke, in addition to a developed set of courses for advanced placement in college. Also, students believed that they had more free time at their disposal at Penbroke High. But, this 'flex' system was under attack for allowing students too much time to hang around the halls and to cause noise which disrupted academic instruction. It was also inconvenient and according to some teachers, it represented an 'ultra left liberal view'. It emphasized freedom at the cost of structure.

There were some long and serious meetings, where many teachers and administrators (these were the department 'directors') spoke, at Penbroke concerning the possibility of at least dealing with the noise in the halls problem. 'Expert' interpersonal communications specialists were called in to consult and facilitate faculty discussions. A popular solution was to have either teachers or the principal and two assistant principals patrol the halls and stop students who didn't have passes. The teacher proposal was jokingly referred to as the 'swat team', and the principals' patrol was called the 'modified swat team'. Swat teams, of course are police gun squads called to the most difficult cases, notably snipers, hostage kidnappers, and other assassins. There was a police television series by the same name. Something needed to be done. 'I, myself', confessed one teacher in a public forum, 'let students out of the cafeteria at 1:02. Five years ago, I would have held them. Yesterday, I made no attempt to hold onto them'. Soon after, there were 'swat teams' used, but there was no consensus about whether they were effective.

Student:	You can't be in the halls during passing time, You can't be . . .
Todd:	Is that new or is that . . .?
Student:	No, well that's newly enforced, it's always been a policy.
Second student:	All of a sudden, they are really cracking down on everything . . . but all these old policies are now being enforced and the kids who have gotten away with these things for three years just can't change all of a sudden.
Philip:	Have things changed since you've been here? Do you see a change in the administration of the school?
Student:	If anything it is looser.
Philip:	How so? could you give me an example?
Student:	The hall policy when I was a freshman was really strictly enforced. I got detention a couple of times. Now you can walk along the hall and most teachers, except for maybe one or two . . .
Philip:	But there has been alot of talk about tightening up the hall policy. Have you heard that?
Student:	A lot of talk, yeah. there has always been alot of talk.
Second student:	Yeah, well for the most part, they don't enforce the hall policy these days.

'Structuring' did proceed, and more students found themselves in one of two structured study halls. In the ninth and tenth grade structured room, there were regularly fifty to sixty structured students. Some students were structured sporadically, usually for 'truancy', as assistant principal Sanguire puts its. In the student definition, 'structure's where they take away your open flexes and you sit in this room'.

Todd:	They make you sit in a room?
Student:	And think about it.
Second student:	You could have 'flex-structure'.
Todd:	What's that?
Student:	Since we run on a flex schedule, instead of two or three days of structure, you could get the whole six day flex schedule for structure.

The structuring of student time in response to incidents of infraction is the least deeply structured aspect of the 'tightening up'. 'Last year', reports a star young teacher, 'we visited a school in Illinois with flex schedule and have now adapted their solution. They have a program which they call the "other program", which is a way of dealing with the deficits of the flex system for those kids who can't handle the freedom and need more structured schedules. Now we have an "other program" and we can keep the flexibility of flex scheduling'. Although most teachers say that they never have discipline problems in their classes, one teacher introduces discussion of the 'other program' with a reference to discipline.

Teacher:	Everybody thinks that Penbroke is so wonderful, all brilliant students, no discipline problems, no reading problems. While it's generally true that the kids here are very college-oriented, we do have a varied student body. . . . We have our discipline problems and have started the other program. I happened to be involved when we started the 'other program' and we found that many students we were getting, about five years ago, I guess, let's say their ability and interest levels were not what we had been getting before . . . And we had to — *we didn't want to lower our standards. We did not want to change flex scheduling*, and so we developed this other program where these students are put into study halls with tutors and people who can help them . . . We felt it was better to contain them and try to help them with their subjects . . .

From both the student and administrators' points of view, the other program is not about ability or interest, but about training in the proper use of time and in the acquisition of more effective self-discipline and self control. 'After all', a student says, 'what life is about is *managing your free time to your benefit'*. According to one of the two assistant principals, Mrs. Cammarado, the problem is largely one of impulse control.

Mrs. Cammarado: When we see a student who can't control that impulse . . . they just continually skip classes and they *really don't have control over themselves,* and it becomes our problem. . . . its a judgment call. If the student is put in a structured study hall and then goes right back to skipping again, that's an alarming sign to me that the kid can't control himself . . . what we're looking for is some kind of growth from the student.

Mrs. Eunly, the orignator of the other program at Penbroke explains her intent:

The original plan was to intervene with students who were not getting work done. Like I have some kids who are really not bad kids, but they just can't get down to work. They're young still, even though they are sophomores and juniors, but they just can't bring themselves to sit down and start to work and for those kids you need someone who will go to them and say 'okay' put the magazine away and let's get the assignment done. They really need alot of specific directions in order to get the thing done. So I have people now who are willing to do that and who understand that that's what it takes sometimes to get these kids to do their work.

Teacher attributions of student motivation rely heavily on theories of the family. The need for the 'other program' is located in the changing demographics of the Penbroke community and in the disruption of family life.

Teacher: I really don't know whether it's — I can't imagine its ability. I think some of it is the change in the community. We have not only houses now. We have alot of apartments going up and I think you're getting a different kind of family in Penbroke and they are are coming into the high school.

The 'other program' teacher, Mrs. Eunly, observes about students in the program:

> The single common element among these students I'm dealing with here, uh, is family. It was astounding last year when I typed a list for parents to see how many parents have different last names from their kids. That's the one element they all have in common.

Beyond 'structuring', of both episodic and systematic varieties, beyond the social reorganization of time, there was a displacement in space, which, for at least some of the Penbroke students (and maybe for us as well) had an especial, symbolic importance. In addition to the award-winning school newspaper, and yearbook, the school's literary magazine, named *The Universe*, was displaced from its office. At Penbroke, offices for student activities are gathering places for group solidarity, spaces where particular interests are shared, and particular identities are confirmed. *The Universe* (a title that may indicate a certain truth to stereo-typical accusations of a self-important snobbery among Penbroke students — which articulate student leaders articulately deny) office was closed, and its inhabitants drifted away to hang out with their less elevated friends who were engaged in putting out the award winning school newspaper.

The official reason for making the *Universe* people homeless was increased this room was needed to help meet state-mandated needs for structuring and tutoring. The student editors' account of displacement from their 'home' in the school is blunt:

Student: There was personal furniture in there — I would say like eight pieces. What they did during the summer was they threw everything out and without warning and they took the office away.

A teacher's account of the event is somewhat more tentative than either the official or student view.

Teacher: I have no idea why the Administration took the *Universe* office away. I may have some ideas, but, certainly, I don't think they'd agree with my ideas.
Philip: About why they lost the office?
Teacher: Yeah, yeah, . . . I think they perceived certain things as going

on in that office, which may or may not be true. I think that
they saw it as a haven for sex, which I don't think was true.
I think they saw it is as way for kids to avoid classes. If you
didn't want to go there, they could just — *that was their
permanent hiding place* — they could just kind of escape to
the *Universe* office. I don' think that was happening. But,
they did need the space — that's a reality. The Administration needed the space, and that's where they took it from,
fortunate or unfortunate as that may be.

The *Universe* people define themselves as 'in opposition', especially to those students who 'are living in their parents country club
style'. They are the *Universe* people who are in conscious opposition,
who consciously try to be different and they are detached.

Student: Do you know what docksiders (style of shoe) are?
Philip: Yes.
Student: Well, people who are different, who are in this *Universe*
            group, are people who consciously and purposively do not
            wear docksiders. *They're intellectuals*.

Later, the magazine was allocated half a room, so-called 'the closet',
which was separated by a thin wall from the toilet. I wrote the following
in my field notes during this period:

One doesn't want to draw too far the analogic importance of
this event. But it seems to me that if you're going to understand the school as a social reality in the present historical
period, then it is not unexpected that some of the events which
occur there are, in some sense, a parallel to events in other
institutional settings.

When the editors of the award-winning school newspaper brainstormed
for their next editorial, one student editor suggested: 'I think what we
should do is do a satire on Reagan's happy family'.

Teachers

The tightening-up of the Reagan restoration was economic as well as
moral. 'Retrenchment' became a popular term in the education industry, and in local school districts, even prosperous ones like Penbroke
that were proud of their schools, communities sought cost-saving

reorganizations, cutbacks and contractions to achieve maximum cost efficiency in schooling. The Penbroke teachers were starting to feel the threat to job security as the community launched a discussion of reorganizing the school district, closing and consolidating schools and of reducing teaching staff. Still, Penbroke teachers had an historical sense of pride in their 'professionalism', in their competence and saw themselves as having the good fortune to be teaching in Penbroke.

One teacher recently taught at Grummitt High School and he compared teaching in the two schools:

> I hated my job at Grummitt. I was going to quit teaching al-together, but then I heard about this job. I was lucky to get it. I really hated Grummitt. There is nothing the least bit similar between the two places . . . At Grummitt, this is a generaliza-tion, but they would work forty hours a week like at McDonalds without the idea of putting it away toward anything. They would buy cars and the current fashions. It is hard for me to relate to something like that . . . I work better with kids like these I can relate to. I went to a high school like this and I grew up in a background similar to this. . . . These people are student ori-ented. The teachers are so much brighter too. They are more worldly. I really love my job here. There is not anything right now that I would rather be doing. . . . At Grummitt, on the other hand, there was no respect, all around. Here, these kids have alot of respect for education and they are polite. This is a rare place . . .

The 'theodicy of good fortune' is widely shared among the teach-ers. 'I'm not sure that you could find a school anywhere in the United States that is nicer than Penbroke', according to a teacher who has taught there for fifteen years. Here are some of the elements of the teachers' beliefs in their 'good fortune':

> The lucky break is that I did get in here . . . the luck of being in a school where there is such a wonderful department . . . I feel competent and respected here . . .

> The kids are nice kids. The faculty — at least those I associate with — are super. You can come out smelling like a rose here. I really like it.

> I consider myself very fortunate because the kids who come to me come because they want to and they are very highly motivated . . .

And it is pleasant; everyone is very nice . . . the working conditions are really very good.

One other thing that I didn't mention is that we are pretty much allowed to teach the way we want to . . . it fosters a creative atmosphere.

I feel fortunate to be a teacher in Penbroke . . . because from what I have heard and read this is a sort of a 'Mecca'. The atmosphere, the environment is very conducive to positive education. . . . I am fortunate to work with the kids I work with. . . . I don't have discipline problems with these kids . . . Its very professional . . .

This is a school where teachers win county and statewide teaching awards. Many teachers are happy not only because of their luck at getting into work at Penbroke, but also because they get to teach elective courses that they enjoy. While most have masters degrees, they continue to go to conferences, read, grade papers on weekends, and despite murmurs of heavy loads, they 'still love the electives'.

There are complaints and stories of teachers who have left to take up other occupations, and of tension and rift between the veteran and newer teachers — at a time where there is still relatively little turnover, because of 'contraction'. The overworked teacher, while complaining that 'it is too much work for too little reward' continues to spend weekends grading papers. But the sense of good fortune is being tempered.

Teacher: I think its going to get worse before it gets better, because the surge of lower enrollment is now high hit in the middle school and in another three or four years, its going to be over here in the high school. And if we go from 1300 or so students down to 1000, well, that's naturally going to affect us a lot.

Second teacher: There isn't much turnover now, hardly any new teachers. Enrollment's going down, so they're not hiring.

Third teacher: I think alot of the younger people are very concerned about losing jobs and things like that, and declining enrollment, I think that's a scary thing for them. I think some of the younger teachers are concerned about making ends meet, unless both people — you know the low man on the totem pole, salary wise, unless there are two salaries coming in.

Fourth teacher: This is the first in a reduction type of thing.

Along with the fear of firings and lay offs that accompanies the professional pride and sense of good fortune to work at Penbroke, teachers reflect on the other side of professionalism: the fragmentation of specialization that manifests itself in a pattern of 'departmentalization'. Departmentalization has the effect of separating teachers from the large collectivity of their colleagues, and of creating strong departmental, rather than school-wide feeling of identity and belonging. Around the core of professional pride there emerges a sense of disconnection, isolation, separateness from the larger society of the school faculty.

The red-brick, white-trimmed building that sits back on a spacious lawn in the heart of the suburb of Penbroke, college-like in its appearance, was inadequate for the growing community and a new wing was added.

Teacher: See, before we added on and did all this, we all ate in the same area. The teachers — if they had any place, it was just their own room. We didn't have a department center . . . But now you see, everybody's got their own little offices and their own areas and so forth, and alot of them eat there, with a few other teachers in the department, and so we're much more departmentalized now than we were then.

When we set up these centers, we knew that it was going to happen and the teachers said: 'Gee, we don't get together enough as it is now, but at least when the teachers used to eat together in that small, dumpy room, over there in the corner . . . nothing like it used to be . . .

One bad thing about this school is that we tend to be *isolated*. We don't really have a central faculty area to get together. We have our centers, and that's where we tend to be, and it kind of leaves you isolated from other members of the faculty. You know, once in a great while . . .

Teacher: I find that since we have had flex scheduling we have be-

> come departmentalized. In other words, the school focuses *in departments rather than as a high school in general.* I don't know if I'm making it clear. But we do tend to stay in our departments.

June: I have never seen a school that has as rigid departmentalization or as highly organized departmentalization and several teachers have told me regardless of what department they are in its like having schools within schools — that it is so hard to have much *communication between teachers as the whole school.*

Teacher: Oh, yes, every department is — we're all competing — it's not nice to say competing — but there are only so many courses and so many people . . .

The very professional specialization and competence that gets realized in a school organized according to subject matter learning centers contributes to the attenuation of social connection among teachers, and to the loss of identification with the school as a whole. The social attenuation that follows this form of professional competence also has curricular implications.

Teacher: We haven't sat down and said what are the common things kids have to learn — that all he has to learn is physics or math, English and so on. Aren't there perhaps more important things like, you know, facing up to life, you know — that is a huge goal. But what does that include, you know, to be able to make decisions, accept failure and so on — attitudinal type things that would make for a richer being. And these, I think, would spring from a long consideration of what the philosophy of the school should be. And I really feel that it's got to go back to that and that's where we'll begin.

Second Teacher: But how about the human qualities in education? The main goal of the high school is to make a better educated citizenry who is more intelligent and who will learn to have better judgment. Instead of emphasizing this, we emphasize instead how happy we are that we have two hundred and forty-something courses . . . First of all, are you aware that it is your responsibility as a human being to care for another

human being? What I am saying is: Why don't we
try to emphasize a little more the human context?

Leadership

Professional specialization at Penbroke, while it provides pride and an
aura of competence, leads — at the very concrete level of physical
arrangement and connection — to a sense of separateness from the
totality of the school. At Grummitt High, the presence of the disciplinary apparatus, and secondarily, sports and theater, offers a compensatory structure to provide identity anchors in the absence of caring
interpersonal relations. At Penbroke, the apparatus at the center is
not forcefully and oppressively present to organize experience and
identity processes. Rather than the forceful presence of Dr. Joe
Kingman, the principal, and Mr. Bech, the self-acknowledged chief of
police, rather than the dessication of caring interaction through excessive rationalization and a cycle of mutual withdrawal, Penbroke
displays a professionalization of the social and a displacement of au-
thoritative leadership by rationalized interpersonalism.

With the absence of identification with the social totality, ritualistic
participation and the ethos of communicative competence substitutes
for society. The hall policy issue and the discussion of 'swat teams'
only partially belong to the 'tightening up'. That faculty meeting also
represented an effort to 'establish a PROCESS', to set up more effective
means of 'decision making' and to heal 'the schism between the teachers
and the administration'. 'The process' is imported into the school via
communication expert consultants, 'trainers' who urge a 'Japanese style
of decision making' on the faculty — taking a long time to achieve
consensus, and then being able to implement actions and policies
quickly. The expert 'trainers' also lead workshops during staff days in
order to develop interpersonal communication skills to help deal with
tensions within the staff. When a new departmental director encounters
resistance and dissension in his department, experts in facilitating
communicative competence are brought in to help resolve conflicts in
the split department.

The expert trainers in interpersonal communication are only
underlining a communicative ethos that already exists at Penbroke.
Student council leaders echo the faculty line that punctuates conversations: 'Let's sit down and talk about it'. Meetings are so prevalent
that one of the school's directors observes, in the rhetoric of interpersonalism, a distinction in *types* of meetings: 'People have expressed

a desire to have substantive meetings and to go beyond routine meetings'. Those who oppose interpersonalism as a solution to the 'tensions', 'stress', 'schism' are labeled the 'right wing' by younger faculty who describe them as embittered.

Teacher: I know that the administrators think that they are making big efforts to make sure . . . (they're not blamed for things). They have workshops on values clarification. I am OK, You are OK — touchy feely stuff.
June: What did you think of that?
Teacher: I didn't go to it, but I heard alot of it and I heard alot of people were angry that they had to be involved in it.

Nevertheless, even the 'right wing' is operating within a faculty culture of interpersonalism — obviously itself not fully consensual — where conversations are punctuated with 'let's sit down and talk about it', and often end with 'well, let's set a meeting'. Calls for further communication, like, 'We need a feedback process. We need to work together', and 'we need to have a discussion' or encouragement for further training in 'decision-making skills' are countered with calls for more 'visible leadership'. The sociey whose center is emptied by professionalism, the 'Noah's ark', a teacher calls it, tries to put it back together with the expert glue of communications. Still failing that, teachers want more active, hands-on leadership. 'The Principal doesn't *act*'. 'He's so very remote', teachers complain. 'He's very nice. And if we sit and have lunch, he'll tell a nice joke and everything. But, if he has a problem, instead of following through, he kind of hopes it will go away by itself'.

Interpersonal training does not create a social center. At the end of liberalism, performance needs make it professionally acceptable to call for a strong leader.

Teacher: I am not alone in feeling that there is a lack of leadership on his part, and that we don't get focus or direction from him . . . he is not as forceful as he should be and does not make decisions that he should be making and that need to be made. I think that sometimes this faculty needs to have someone say you will or you will not do this, that or the other. You know, I don't think he has to be nasty about it, but I think this or any faculty needs to know that there is somebody who is firmly in charge of the ship of state and I do not get that impression here.

June:	Your descriptions make him sound like a faceless corporate leader.
Todd:	Have you seen Dr. Snowbridge alot?
June:	I have seen him once since I've been here.
Todd:	Really
June:	He's just — they all talk about him as the "missing principal" or the 'phantom principal'.
Todd:	You know, at Grummitt, its not like that . . . The principal is the most visible person in the school . . . You know that it's his school and he is . . .
June:	He just likes all that contact all the time with people — completely different style. Here, it's like a corporation, and he's the president, up on the nineteenth floor.

Some teachers believe that the school is ruled by committees. It is a very cumbersome and slow moving way to do it. It seems to be working though.

For others, the problem is not one of leadership, but of the character of the faculty: 'Our real problem is that we are all very bright and we're all educational leaders and it's difficult for us to be peons at a meeting'.

Lack of leadership seems a fitting complement to lack of structure as the post-liberal diagnosis of 'lack of focus', or 'erosion of authority'. Another element in this story of slippage within an ambience of professional pride and achievement is the failure of families to provide the right balance of relationship to the school.

Parents: Teachers' View

Parents problems that affect school life are either excessive involvement in their children's academic schoolwork or insufficient involvement and disruption and distraction because of 'family problems'. Parents are either too much or too little involved in their children's school lives. Teachers see parental 'pressure' and 'success desire' as interferring with their professional work:

In Penbroke, these (troublesome) parents are catered to . . . they make such a big stink over some little thing and everyone bows to them, you know, 'what can we do? what can be taken care of?' Minor things that are unimportant are important here; but major things such as vandalism . . . they don't even consider it . . . a minority of parents completely control this school and the administration is so wishy washy that they just cater to these people. . . .

June: What do you think the other constituencies are besides parents being catered to?

Teacher: Kids become very demanding and if a kid wants something he will get it — no matter which teacher he steps on. In some respects, the kid is right and the teacher is wrong.

June: So you say that there are some kids who challenge authority?

Teacher: I don't necessarily know if it's authority — just challenging in general, their peers too. More or less the whole world. There is a great deal of parental pressure on the kid to succeed and get involved in activities . . . they have the pressures of college to succeed . . . The demand for success is there. The expectation is there for the community. There is parental involvement here on a scale which sometimes they tread into my decision-making.

Elaine: What does this parental push mean for the student?

Teacher: Well, in my case it means wonderful students. I have academic, aggressive, prepared, enthusiastic students.

Teacher: The phone calls that I will get from parents who want me to make special cases for their children. It is OK in the aggregate, but when it comes down to their little sweetheart, they want what they want and I could avoid confrontation by giving it to them, but I won't do it. I couldn't remain a professional.

June: Well, the assistant principal says that if you screw up, the parents will let you know immediately, and if you don't — if a kid has done something wrong or has failed to achieve, you'd better have everything in place before the parent comes in or they'll kill you.

It is the preoccupied, undercommitted parent who now looms larger on the horizon of Penbroke teachers' problems.

Teacher: There's been a tremendous amount of change here during the past fifteen years. We get more people. I won't say exactly blue collar workers — well, I don't know, less professional people. . . . you know, its not all magnificent homes . . . we have people moving here because we have great support ser-

	vices. . . . So, we're getting alot of kids who have problems or who are not great learners. So you have to gear the school towards them too . . . so you're lowering your standards so that everybody can achieve to some point. So, you're not getting the fine quality from the top people — not what they're capable of . . . some of these kids come from broken homes, and some of them are even culturally deprived . . . including not having any books in the home.
Second Teacher:	If you look at those kids regardless of whether they are low ability, alot of it has to do with what happens at home. A greater number of separated families and I don't think that a week goes by that I don't talk with the kid where I learn that there is a separation in their family or a second marriage and the kid is having trouble with that. The four drops that I have had this year have been because the parents were fighting with one another and in one case they pulled the kid out of school because they couldn't agree. . . . I want to argue this point — that the students who dropped my courses, failed my courses, come from family situations that are in trouble. There is alot of animosity there. Something like the security of their home being threathened. I mean that's a terrible thing for them.

Mrs. Eunly talks about the students in the 'other program':

So, typically, I think what we are seeing are kids whose parents are not being deliberately neglectful but who are under pressures of their own and so they either avoid or don't have time or don't give the kids enough support because of their own problems. That seems to be what's going on. . . . Well, for them it isn't rosey, I think.

This is the 'human', historical context in which the students at Penbroke are trying to become somebody, trying to succeed.

Student Life in the Professional Middle Class: Success

Penbroke is a school renowned for the academic successes of its students. They not only go to college, but they go to the very best colleges. This year, of the ten students in the county accepted at Harvard, four were from Penbroke. They don't all get accepted, but they expect to go to Princeton, Dartmouth, and Brown; Cornell and Vassar are second choices. Of course, a small percentage of students will go to the local community college or a branch of the state university. But that is not what Penbroke is about for most students.

Students, teachers, and guidance counselors all talk about the 'pressure to succeed', to get very good grades, score high on the national standardized tests and to get into one of the best colleges. Children's success in school is part of a wider set of status competitions among parents in the community. Students know that their parents are not alone in pushing them to succeed.

Student: So it is alot of pressure.

Elaine: Do you think your parents are unusual in that?

Student: No, I think my parents are — well they expect alot from me but I know my friend's parents — last year, all of the years before finals — she wasn't allow to go out three weeks before finals because she had to sit home and study and she has a brother who is married and went to Yale and he is a surgeon . . . OK, now there is my friend and she is the youngest, OK? — and her parents expect her — and she is brilliant. She is going to Princeton, but all of those years before no one knew she was going to Princeton and her parents made her you know, sit home and study and my parents aren't like that, but then again. . . . In Penbroke, in general, people are brought up in that way.

The same student continues:

Well, what I mean when I say strong personality — I mean you have to have a strong personality to be able to handle the pressure because sometimes it gets really intense . . . there's always the pressure to be well-rounded so, oh, you have to do this so you can get into college and you have to do that so you can get into college. The whole purpose of going to school is so you can get into college, which is stupid. It is really dumb . . . that is why I like summer so much; (school) work is just a drag.

One of the disappointed seniors who will have to go to Cornell rather than his first choice of Harvard, reflects back on the parental influence in success orientation.

Also there is a great deal of seventeen going on thirty five. We have been *trained to be precocious from stage one through our parents* and the professional and university parents and so many others. We have always been taught to *abandon childhood, go ahead*, form more advanced and subtle forms of thinking . . . at this stage it is sort of everyone — this is just my thinking — they have been taught to go ahead and now we are at the stage where we should be going ahead. Everyone is now sort of looking back saying — 'Wait a minute. What was gone? What did we miss?'

Teachers generally appreciate their 'highly motivated' students who do not present discipline problems and who like to 'pack their schedules with advanced placement courses'. But, they are aware that their 'good fortune' in having this type of student carries with it some costs.

Teacher: I have freshmen who come in and they want — they say that they have to go to a certain college, a specific college, often one that Mom or Dad went to, and they have to get good grades. Well, you know, this is ninth grade and they are worrying about when they apply in the twelfth grade. But this is how oriented these kids are. They are definitely geared for good grades and getting into good colleges and this kind of thing. I think that's the majority in this school — they were brought up that way.

Second Teacher: There is a great deal of parental pressure on the kids to succeed and get involved in activities and many times I think one of the problems alot of kids have is that they're involved in too many things at one time and they have all these things pulling at them from one direction and that creates, I think, problems for many youngsers who attend school here. Everyone agrees that this is 'a pre-college school' and that there is serious competition for grades.

Third Teacher: Well, their goals are not the same as our goals. I mean my goal is that they develop an understanding of what's going on in the world. Their goal is to get a good grade. . . . Well, this year, I'm teaching

> an enriched section for the first time.... Uh, those
> kids, more than any others, are in it for the grade.
> They're in pretty tough competition ... there's alot
> of parental pressure on them.

Students report both the pressure and the competitiveness.

Student: There's pressure from parents, especially college
time, pressure from parents, pressure from teachers,
pressure from friends who are doing better than you,
when you know that you can do better than they are
doing. Pressure, competitiveness with your own ca-
pabilities, I think ... *I'm very loaded down.*

Second Student: I don't like high school — high school is not fun, but
it is something I have to do because I'm going to
college ... I've known that I'm going to college since
I was seven ... I've been told — since I can remember — that I will be bright. That I am bright.... Well,
you know, they pushed Sesame Street on me since
I can remember.

The student response is to compete, to prepare for college, to
achieve grades:

Elaine: I went to a guidance meeting where the counselor did a values
clarification thing where one was highly competitive and the
other end was where you would do anything to avoid competition. All but two out of the fifteen students placed themselves on the high end. Some said that they would be willing
to kill to win.

Students can be very direct about the competition: 'It was my friends
who did better than I on this test. But it was my friends, and still, I felt
mad at them'.

Todd: Are you just as competitive as other people?

Student: You have to be really. You are kind of drawn into it. You
are *either down and not bothered about it or you are in the
competitiveness.*

In the cosmology of success, sin is failure to achieve.

Student: ... but if I think I can get an A and I get a B, I'm disappointed in myself. Underachieving isn't good. A lot of my

friends are under-achievers. [And then, more forcefully] I've had good teachers and I've had bad teachers, but either way, it's not an excuse for doing poorly in class, *that's the biggest sin of all.*

In these conditions, students value the flex schedule since they believe that it teaches them how to manage their time — a central prerequisite for success in college. 'We're getting good preparation for college-learning on how to use our time'. Time-management, as part of the self-discipline and self-control, developmental 'growth' ideals, while valued as a 'college survival skill' does not adequately deflect, at least for some students, the sense that they have no time and that their *schedules* are 'packed' or that they are 'loaded down'. Even academically successful students can be sardonic about the centrality of scheduling in their lives, albeit flex scheduling:

Student: If I have time for and I'm free, oh yea, World Holocaust; I'll think about it. I mean ... it's almost like, 'wow' if they dropped the bomb and I wasn't free — it's like, *I have to try to fit everything into my schedule.* And college, I guess, will be just like that.

Cynical humor is one way to manage the 'intense pressure' to succeed. As the students say, others are 'down about it'. Teachers observe HOW students get down about it.

June: How does it all come out?
Teacher: It come out in kids having nervous breakdowns — getting ulcers. Some of them just keep working, but they are very depressed. Others give up and become trouble makers. They wind up being sent away.
Second Teacher: There is a lot of that here — of kids who see other people doing so well that they say I can't do that and they give up or they are so pressured that they decide the heck with you — I am going to screw up ... there is alot of that and there is alot of the other thing where kids really do knock themselves out but sometimes they just can't be as good as the other ones are and it is very frustrating.

Fear of the sin of 'underachievement' also leads to over-expectation.

Teacher: This is the point at which a kid will say to you can I take this course and you have to say 'No. You can't take that course — that would be too hard for you'. That is hard because some of them don't recognize their limitations. Some of them will say, 'I think I would like to take AP' — a kid who is in a basic level class and who can't write a sentence and you have to explain to her that AP is really for superior students who are going to get college credit now and it is hard. . . . It is an unpleasant thing you have to face day after day to help a person with that and it is sad, and yet that is reality.

June: What about the 'other program'?

Teacher: The kids in the 'other program' are not necessarily learning disabled and many of them are in fact quite bright but they are for one reason or another perhaps *emotionally incapable of conforming to the system or using flex properly.*

Average achievement, neither AP nor the other program leads to a sense of failure. A teacher recounts particular students experience:

This student ran away. It was a tense couple of days, but she came back and talked to her parents and said: 'Look, you're both lawyers. I'm just a normal kid. I feel very inadequate in this school. I want to leave this school and go someplace else. I feel that you're both successes and that I'm failing you because I'm getting a B in a course'. . . . She feels very inadequate. She's a talented girl and she feels as though she's a failure . . . Uhm, I think kids who aren't getting stroked by their teachers for doing well in terms of grades aren't saying much because they're kind of outcasts, but they have very low self-esteem.

The student side of the same experience is portrayed more graphically:

My GPA (grade point average) is pretty low, so, while I hang aound with some of the smarter kids in school, my grades and the things I'm doing are often just behind. So I often feel like *I'm always behind the power curve* . . . I feel like I have to catch up to them . . . that the thing . . . I'm struggling to stay up where I don't belong.

Student: I always got A's and my parents never had to worry about it and my younger brother comes home with a report card and there aren't any C's, but there aren't any A's either. It is sort of — he feels really bad. But the average person — I don't think there is really much opportunity for an average person at this school . . . It doesn't seem like this is a normal average school. I don't know.

Some students have it 'all mapped out' as Becky observes: 'She has it all straight in her head, where she was going . . . Everything she did and everything she talked about . . . She had it all figured out — *every aspect of her life*, and why just having a good time was important'. Others reject the future orientation of success, and the fully rationalized — 'all mapped out' — organization of their life course. To them, the well-packed and well-managed, college-oriented schedule of good grades and good time management leads to a certain death of the present, an emptiness of everyday life.

Among these dissenters are 'the intellectuals' or *Universe* people; others are from among the small group of kids who hang out in the backyard, the 'yarders', who, more like Grummitt high school rads, and others are 'normals', disillusioned with the fast, future-directed pace of student life for success at Penbroke.

Student: When I came to Penbroke, I thought that they were all robots. They wore the same clothes and I'm here in my jeans and t-shirt and here they are in their 'docksiders' . . . And, oh my God, they're all alike. And I hung around with these snobby stuck-up people for a while because I didn't know anybody. Then I came down to earth and realized that these people aren't like me. Not just people whose ENTIRE MIND dwells with what they are going to do when they get out of high school. Of course, it's something to think about . . . They don't live their life day-by-day. They live by the future . . . And a lot of their parents give them hassles.

Several years ago, in order to bring the 'yarders' into the school, the Administration established the 'Public', a room on the first floor with some carpeting and chairs, as a student lounge. At first, the Public was yarder territory, and known as a smokers and druggies hangout. Over the years, the population of the Public room changed; intellectuals, preppies and jocks took over the Public. With the new enforcement effort, more students are crowding into the Public. With its glass window providing easy visibility to outsiders, the Public, observes Elaine, 'looks like a nursery'. Students listen to piped in music in the Public, and because they have broken the 'no eating and no grafitti rule', the public is sometimes closed for collective self-discipline — until the student council can work out a 'process' for eliminating rule violators from the Public space. Meanwhile, the Public becomes more crowded as the halls tighten up and students begin lobbying for a 'Public after dark', to accomodate the increased demand for a public social meeting place. Social groups or 'cliques' sit separately in the Public; but it is a place where there are students from most social quarters sitting in the same place.

Philip: Sometimes, it feels stifling to me here. It feels like there is no life being lived here. I keep wondering where do the kids live their lives and I asked them that and they said that it was a dull town and a dead place. . . . Life goes on and now that the halls are getting tighter . . .

Elaine: They are all shifting to the Public or the cafeteria.

'Look around the Public', a student directs me. 'You see that girl over there? Docksider shoes, whale belts. They wear barrettes in their hair. And they're all dressed and their noses in the air . . . three layers of shirts, Izods (brandname), turtleneck and sweater shirt. . . . 'There is inter-group animosity at Penbroke, and while it is not as intense as the individual competition for academic success, it can evoke strong feelings. 'See that girl? I'd like to throw up on her'.

Group life is portrayed as 'materialistic', and like grade success, out of reach for many 'normal' people:

Student: Everybody is pretty much conceited, but yet they care what everybody else thinks about them. Do you know what I am saying? PEOPLE ARE VERY INTO THEMSELVES. Like it is my own little world. I am so great. I am so beautiful. I know everybody loves me. My hair is perfect. I get it cut ten times a week. But they also feel they have to look great for everybody to look at me. Do you know what I am saying?

Yeah. Did you notice that everybody here — *nobody is wearing anything really out of the ordinary*. You can see that right? There are oxfords and jeans and sweaters . . . but nobody is really wearing anything out of the ordinary. You don't see any really weird clothes because if

you wear really weird clothes here, your reputation goes
down.

Todd: So it's materialistic type of —

Student: This school is so materialistic. If you don't have a Cadillac
or BMW, it is like man, don't hang out with me. For people
like me, normal, in-between people, there's nothing here for
me. . . . Penbroke is geared for those brilliant and beautiful
people. . . . And then the rest of us kind of fade into the
background, you know, you're just the kids who are taking
regular this or that . . . and the teachers don't usually enjoy
teaching those courses.

The competitive, academic, college-acceptance life course at
Penbroke leads to a sense of failure and inadequacy, not only among
the 'normals', but also among some of the *Universe* people, and some
other students who defensively describe themselves as being 'snobby
and elitist'. Life at the top is not satisfying to some of its most articulate
intiates.

Student: I don't think some of them really know what's going on, and
when people think, you know, all this time they've been
told that they are on the top, they are the best, and now
people are saying you're not, and they're very insecure about
it. And when I start doing things that I want to do, like
dressing differently or acting differently, it scares them
I think.

There are students who believe that tomorrow will be 'bigger and
better' and that when they finish school, they will be able to begin to
live more broadly and, to consider larger social questions. There are
students who describe life at Penbroke not in terms of pressure or the
absence of a lived life in the here and now, but in the language of
'realism' and goal-orientation. There are students who assert that the
purpose of school is for them to achieve more than their parents, to
'go higher'. But more often, when we discuss the future, they fear that
they will not be able to achieve their parents standard of living, their
success. By then, houses in Penbroke will cost almost a quarter of a
million dollars.

Seniors, those students who teachers talked about as thinking of
their grades for that 'certain college' already in the ninth grade, are in
the best position, however, to articulate the disappointment and the
failure not in a course or two, but in their life's career trajectory — not

measuring up to the standards of the world beyond Penbroke, where they must ultimately validate their success.

Student:	... What did we miss?
Philip:	So there is a feeling that you have sort of missed something?
Second Student:	I would say that most of our group feels a little bit inadequate.
Philip:	In what way?
Student:	We are not happy.
Second Student:	We weren't really socially active.
Student:	Sort of like axed. You are not miserable.
Second Student:	And what it is — it doesn't exist at all. It is an illusion.
Philip:	What is happiness?
Second Student:	This dream — like I wanted to go to Harvard and I didn't get in. *I wanted it desperately*, but I did not get in.
Student:	Same here. Not with Harvard, but with ...
Philip:	So did you get into other schools?
Second Student:	Yeah, we got into other schools.
Philip:	Those are nice places, I think. You are not happy?
Second Student:	We are not particularly happy.
Student:	*We have to get psyched down* to go to those schools. My God — these are excellent schools. They are top rank, but mentally for us there is sort of like.
Second Student:	It is a click below what we expected.
Student:	The thing is you are leaving the elite now ... you get the feeling that you are not the top. The fact is that the top has become too big for you.
Second Student:	Yea. It is a downward movement. It is an *incredibly downward movement*.
Student:	One of my major problems is that now we have to prove ourselves. We have to work that much harder ... it was within the jaws of victory.

This sense of failure of 'downward movement' is one of the costs of ambition at Penbroke. Among the faculty there are teachers who simply nod their heads in wonderment about student life, as they utter: 'For them it is always, succeed, succeed, succeed. ...' Others are less accepting:

I think that this school is overly academic conscious. They are
all too bent on taking AP courses and getting advanced placement credit in college. They are too concerned with their grades.
Time after time you give someone a B+ and they really deserve
a C and they raise such a stink. You call the parents and the
Administration gets into it and the kid says I want an A and
they end up getting it. . . . How much more of a learning experience could that be? No — they don't have time for that
in their schedules. The kids are passing all those tests, but they
have no idea what's in that. You can train a parrot to say all
kinds of words, but they don't know when to say them. I don't
think these kids will do better in college than kids from some
other local high schools. They aren't any different.

More empathically, a guidance counselor offers a wishful solution: 'I
wish I had a magic way of making the kids feel less pressured'.

... Without Society

Students at Penbroke have friends and a social life. They 'hang out',
go to parties, and participate in extra-curricular activities, like the
model UN Club, where they prepare for academic competitions with
other high schools. Students participate in theatrical productions, go
to athletic events, join clubs and a few even went on a school trip
abroad. Still, there is a feeling among many students and teachers that
something is missing at Penbroke, something is absent at the center of
its collective life.

   In my view, it is the social center that is absent at Penbroke; a
center so lacking that students acknowledge that even when they
participate, they do not identify beyond the particular activity. There
is not simply an absence of identification with a social center; there is
recognition of an absence, and a yearning to fill it. The students, like
the teachers, are fragmented into areas of interest. Just as the teachers
are 'departmentalized' and have lost a sense of common collective
membership while in the pursuit of professional competence and
specialization; so too the students, while pursuing grades and superior
college entrance, while trying to cope with the competition of the high
expectations held for them and which they come to hold for themselves
unwittingly surrender the social totality of the school. More than a
future-oriented elipsis of life in the everyday social present and more
than a competitive infringement on the building of social solidarities,

what is lost and yearned for is the very idea that there is a social whole.

Students express this absence at the center by saying that there is no 'school spirit', or more often by openly stating — even defensively boasting of — their 'apathy'. Social life in the Public room, windowed, visible, nursery-like, chaos-seeming ghetto for student culture, intensifies, at the same time that there is an intractable resistance to participation in the *organized* social life of the school. At the same time, there occurs in Penbroke High School a new and high wave of vandalism, a vandalism so pervasive that it replaces the sale and use of drugs as a major concern of 'the Administration', teachers, and those 'responsible' students who monitor collective self-monitoring through student organizations like the student council.

Forums are held to discuss the vandalism and a financial incentive is established as a deterrent. A lump sum of a thousand dollars is set aside for vandalism repair. The incentive is that all money not used in this 'vandalism fund' will be given to students for student activities. But, students say that they don't need the 'incentive': 'We have money coming out our ears'. Teachers ruminate about the student apathy and the vandalism, and even they are unwilling to attribute the social problems of the school to the 'yarders' or to the few minority, inner city youths bussed into Penbroke in a residual program from the liberal time before the restoration began. Instead, they acknowledge that the problems of apathy and vandalism have something to do with the core of school life, that they are consequences of the prevailing mainstream activities and not dismissible aberrations.

Most kids at Penbroke, anyone will tell you, are nice, polite, intelligent, reasonable and also, sophisticated and competent, independent and responsible. Teachers who have taught elsewhere are so pleasantly surprised about how one can work with them, assume they will take responsibility and work successfully to accomplish goals. Sophistication stands out. Our research team was incredulous, after spending some months at Grummitt, and then coming to Penbroke, to discover not only the general sophistication of the students, but their ability to reflectively articulate their lives, to abstract from their lives and recast experience into theoretical and impersonal terms. In a word, 'it's just professionalism', a teacher remarks, 'and that professional attitude is what really amazed me when I came to teach here'. These students know how to work alone, without direct and continuous adult supervision. They are responsible. But what are they responsible for?

They are responsible for making particular activities, extra-curricular or clubs successful. Usually, these are academically related, and while they do reflect student interests, they are in a sense 'credit-bearing' for college applications. Collective activities that represent the whole school, however, go poorly attended; they are not good investments. But, the distribution of activity is not simply a rational goal-oriented calculation. Rather, it is that, like the teachers, the path and commitment of everyday life is toward rational individual, instrumental, career-oriented, 'departmentalized' or specialized, achievement. The entire course of student life leads to the occlusion of the social totality that is represented by the school and by school spirit. Vandalism is a marginal activity, and partly expresses a need for public representation; some of the vandalism is grafitti. Some of the vandalism is highly specialized and instrumental; scales used in the chemistry lab are stolen — the sort of scales people use to weigh drugs, to subdivide and package for sale. But, some of the vandalism is defacement and destruction. It is directed against the school itself, against the 'idea of the school', as one student put it.

This absence of the larger society, the withholding of energies from activities that represent the totality may in part be just good 'managing of your free time'. Teachers believe that more than that is at issue.

Teacher: As pleased as I am to be working in this district, I think that there is a lack of community in Penbroke as far as the teachers and the students are concerned ... Students are terrible. There is really a *real lack of community*. When I went to school everyone would go to the football games or to the basketball games, the musical, there were dances. *The school was the center of my life, I don't think that is true here* ... If you have gone to the meetings about the reorganization, you have heard them talk about the sense of community here in Penbroke. I think that they are full of baloney ... I see this as a very splintered community. ... I don't see community support for the teams or the musicals. I may be wrong, but I think that it is our mess. We are in it together. I don't see alot of effective communication. ...

Another teacher recounts her experience at another, less prestigious high school and compares it to Penbroke.

Teacher: Yeah, intellectually I think in terms of my teaching career that these students here at Penbroke are probably the most gifted I've worked with ... In the small community that I came from, the students weren't anywhere near as gifted, but as human beings they were far higher or the totem pole than the Penbroke kids. One of the frustrations that I have with my kids here is that number one there is a tremendous amount of apathy here, just in terms of the school and school spirit and this kind of thing. . . . they are very grade conscious. And very college bound, you know, the Ivy League ten, the big ten schools. You know, you mention State University to alot of these kids around here and they say — 'Oh my god, that's the end of the world. . . .

June: That's the last resort. Uhm, I wonder about the lack of emotionalism. I can't quite put my finger on it . . . I even get that from people who teach hard science, they wonder too about the lack of spontaneity, if you will . . .

Teachers on apathy:

Teacher: We don't have any discipline or behavior problems. They are there but they are not disruptive. I have never had a disruption in my class that didn't evaporate.

June: Yeah, it looks much more orderly than almost any school environment that I have ever been in . . .

Teacher: We don't have antagonism between the faculty and the student body. But we don't have that kind of SOCIAL THING. We don't have school spirit either . . . I dont know. . . . I think that youngsters here — their social life is not tied to the high school as much as socializing youngsters elsewhere. . . . People don't go to games. They don't go to dances. They don't go to social functions they don't raise money for their senior class.
We have very low percentage participation in our club. Here there are too many other activities that the kids get involved in outside of school — jobs and shopping and movies and things that they have access to in a city and they don't in rural environment . . . And school is not the major source of entertainment . . . they've got museums, and concerts and sports activities outside of school and all kinds of things that the school can't compete with.
They're missing out. I think that's the major reason why we have virtually no school spirit in this school. At a football game, you may get a hundred and fifty people (less than ten per cent of the student population). A basketball game

there's a — you know, you don't get very many people. Two years ago we had a very strong ice hockey team and they made it to the play-offs ... uhm, once they made it and had proven themselves, then people started to flock to the games. It was like they wanted to be associated with a winner. It didn't have anything to do with going because it was part of our school.

Students are more pointed in the view that even collective social activity is specialized, and not 'part of our school' — not a representative action of commitment to collective identity.

Student: When they join groups or activities, it is not for the school but for that activity. They feel loyal to that activity. They are not apathetic. *They are apathetic to the idea of the school.*

Students do attribute the 'apathy' to an excessively instrumental emphasis on college preparation, grades, and the attendant competition.

Student: I think that everybody has the general idea that everybody is apathetic ... I really can't say too much about it, but I guess that all of the pressure could contribute to it. .... The competition for good grades so you can get into the good schools.

Active students bemoan the absence of participation in collective activity.

They say that is why they are so bored — because they can't have this and they can't have that. It is because we can't have it because if we do — if we finally get up and have something — *nobody shows up. or we have something and they ruin it by vandalism.*

Student: Homecoming was just a disaster. There was no class spirit or anything.
June: Has it been fun being in this school? Has it been interesting and fun?
Student: No. It's just like a place to go. You get up in the morning ... It's always the same, everyday. There's nothing really different one day after another. I mean, nobody really gets

involved in any of the activities. I mean, even if you put up a poster for something, NOBODY GOES. It's the same thing everyday, I find.

One reason students give for non-involvement is that being too involved, too readily participant shows that you are 'not cool'. 'Cool' requires a certain level of reticence, a style of reserve. 'Everybody is talking about how boring this school is'. After an account of a party, with very poor turnout, he explained the no-shows this way: 'They are *too cool*, I guess'.

'Cooling' or 'mellowing out' is one way to cope with the pressures:

As time went on . . . I turned from a nervous person to a really calm person. You know like things did not affect me then or now. If I hear anything bad about anything, grades or anything, I just say to myself: 'Well that is the way it is'. If I don't get all bent if I am really glad about something, I don't usually jump up and down and go yeah or you know, whatever. I just — whatever happens to me I just look at it and say that is the way it is.

The same sort of self-control of emotion as a response to uncertainty and things that are 'less pleasant' goes beyond grade coping to a means of dealing with the wider world.

And you know, I can think about things that I do care about, but I have gotten to the point where there are not very many things. . . . Like I don't care too much about politics . . . I don't listen to the news a lot because if you listen too much, you get depressed . . . And I think that things are actually a lot better now than in the 1960s with the war and racial tensions and you never know . . . I would rather think pleasant thoughts, like where I am going to college.

One of our team recounted his experiences with Penbroke students in this way:

We talked about school spirit, Penbroke spirit. There is no such thing as Penbroke school spirit. They said now the spirit is for the activity itself. If you are working on the newspaper or the drama club, it is newspaper or drama club spirit rather than school spirit. They said that it is *totally eroded — the Penbroke High School spirit is nothing*. I asked why and they mainly feel that they are *packaged for school, college* and there is a tremendous amount of processing of students, and I think they can feel that. They do not give back anything to the school.

Apathy may be a way, as one student put it, of fighting the school. 'We don't fight them physically, but we fight them cerebrally'. Apathy is a response also to an environment perceived, like the teacher's characterization of the principal, as 'remote, as distant and aloof'. 'There's really not much sympathy in this school . . . the administration is very cold . . . they're just very structured about how things are supposed to run . . . The reputation is running downhill . . . the top people are being drained off to Saddle Ridge High School . . . the Public is getting more and more crowded every year'.

Vandalism recognizes the totality of the school; it is not directed against particular departments (except perhaps in the stealing of laboratory scales). There are varying reports about the vandalism, but the consensus among students and teachers is that it consists in more than graffiti.

Teacher: What they're stealing from us are scales. And we know what they're used for — they're used to weigh up dope. And they probably bring big prices. The electronic scales they stole — it cost us probably fifteen, seventeen hundred dollars. And on the market they can still get five or six hundred dollars for it. . . . We'll order five new ones and they'll steal. The other vandalism we get is that they break walls, or tear up lockers, or throw stink bombs. Some of the kids are having problems at home. And they want to lash out at something, so they lash out at the school.

Todd: The vandalism that's going on — is it just lockers being broken into or. . .?

June: Or tearing up offices, you know, coming in at night and tearing up offices. I'll show you a report.

Teacher: They had Janey in here this morning for trying to torch the school.

Becky: What?

Teacher: They were burning posters off the walls . . . I said what are you doing and she said 'nothing'. The posters were on fire. They have too much freedom.

Todd: Has the vandalism fund deterred anything?

June: Well, obviously not, if anything, it has gotten worse.

Teacher: The vandalism fund is a joke . . . there is zero punishment. This is change, they carry it around and we're talking about a six hundred dollar a month vandalism fund? These kids laugh at it . . . it's ridiculous.

The vandals are 'lashing out' at the school and there are competing causal attributions.

There is a real problem with vandals and lack of respect in the school and those things are not being addressed. I can't really understand the vandalism. When I see a particularly vicious kind of vandalism, it is very hard for me to believe that there isn't some feeling about a system and institution . . . uhm, that there is something up there as an adversary.

Oh, I think an awful lot of these kids who are causing all the vandalism and so on and so forth at the school, are causing that vandalism because they themselves don't feel good about themselves and the reason that they don't feel good about themselves is that they've been pushed into the background, or something like that, because maybe they're not as bright as some others.

Todd: Do you think — what reasons could you give — why do people want to vandalize the school?

Student: I don't know. Mayby they're mad at something. They just feel unhappy.

Teacher: Just as with everything else, we have a tendency to smoothe it over for public image or whatever other reason. I am not sure what the problems are. They are here.

In the student life at Penbroke, there are already all the elements of the social psychology of the professional middle class. Beyond the psychology of striving for success and the methods of cooling out or 'becoming calm' or emotionally self-controlled, there is the dynamic of the emptying of the social center in pursuit of professional competence. I believe that is the common meaning in the departmentalization of the teachers and their efforts at compensatory sociality either through expert-regulated interpersonalism or in the yearning for a strong leader and in the early careerized lives of the students. In both cases, it is the 'idea of the school', in other words, the possibility of a totality and a relation to it (Ashley, 1990) that is being emptied in the professionalized achievement process. In both cases too, the parents are brought in and their influence underlined in what I think is an unintended deflection from the internal dynamic of the school. Of course, the community ethos and its implementation in Penbroke High, makes a difference for school life. But, it is at once the more internal and larger dynamic of the school — its immersion in the rationalizing logic of professionalism — that finally makes the difference.

At Grummitt, 'nobody cares'. In a spiral of mutual withdrawal, the core social relation between teacher and student is eviscerated and overlain with a social regulation that combines state bureaucratism and the back-slapping personalist authority of the principal/boss. At Penbroke, some social relations are attenuated, but it is a centered social totality that gets dissipated in a professional rationalization that appeals to excellence and competence rather than force and rule for its legitimacy. The result is a de-socialization at a deeper level, closer to the social core, which is the possibility of representing and becoming part of the social whole. Any hope, such as that of Barbara Ehrenreich (1989), that this class segment can provide leadership for society is dashed with every reduction in its collective incapacitation to imagine and identify with society. Professionalism is accomplished at Penbroke, but at the price of the society in which it must be embedded.

Chapter 4

The Urban Under-Class: I AM Somebody

Self Dynamics

George Washington High School stands like a fortress, occupying a square block in a neighborhood that has hosted waves of immigrants to All American City since before the turn of the century. Now, most of the students are African-Americans; many of them children of immigrants from southern states to All American City. Students whose parents or grandparents emigrated from Puerto Rico are the second largest ethnic bloc at the school, followed by a small group of Southeast Asian immigrant children. There is a small segment of 'white' students. But, as one student puts it, perhaps hyperbolically, in her reflection on the school:

Student: See, Washington is set up like this — Blacks and Puerto Ricans hang and whites are eliminated.
Philip: They are excluded you mean?
Student: They are a different class, different language, their background is different.

Washington has a bad reputation. One of the store owners in the adjacent blocks where the Washington students 'hang' represents the stereotypical bad reputation version of who is at Washington High School:

What it is — Washington is the melting pot for all the riff raff — all of the bad neighborhoods, the lowest class life, the Puerto Rican, Blacks, all of the bad neighborhoods, the ghetto kids. They are all in one school, which tends to make it bad.

Most Washington students know that the school has a 'bad reputation'. A few think that the reputation is deserved.

Philip: I am trying to understand what the lives of the kids are like in different high schools in different parts of All American City.

Student: Well, you have found the worst school.

Second Student: You have come to the right place.

The majority believes that the reputation is undeserved, a stereotype that their own experience at the school has disspelled.

Student: Yeah. If you have been around as long as I have or anybody really, I must tell you alot of people say Washington is a bad school, terrible school. Some say good. They liked it. But, in my opinion, I love Washington because it is where I have been. It is where I grew up at and I have been going here for years. I know all of the teachers. I have been good. They all respect me and Washington is a decent school.

Second Student: I know you have heard some talk about Washington and I don't know if you were shaky or not, but some people are shaky coming to Washington. When they come in Washington, like I say, they were definitely changed. I don't know if you thought Washington was a bad school or not. When you come and see what Washington is really about I know that changed you right then. If you had any negative thoughts you would have changed right there and then. You know, Washington is not what people are saying. I am talking about the bad kinds of people.

Students want the record set straight, and derogatory attributions made about the school cleared up.

Student: I want it to be classified like any normal school. Our skills and our academic work might not be classified as high as some suburban schools, *but we want it to be known that we are not bad.*

But we want it to be known that we are friendly ... We just have to show them — show them that we are good and not as they say. . . . In my opinion, it's a great place. You see alot of different people of different backgrounds, not all rich and not all poor. Different backgrounds, you know. Interesting and friendly people.

Yeah. Like a teacher was beat up the year before I came by one of the students and you never found out who it was and the papers had it blown up that Washington was all bad and there was no good in it, but I find it different myself. I don't know, school can be what you want it to be and if you try, and you know, you'll turn out better at the end or your grades will . . . there's alot of smart kids here and alot of kids that try. . . .

Even the 'smart kids' at Washington have something to prove. They have to prove that they are 'good, not bad', that they are worthwhile, that they can achieve, that they have respect, that they are decent, that they can have something of their own, that they can make it, 'get over the system' and that they can be somebody. Student life at Washington, from the students' point of view is, at best, a testing ground in self-determination and at worst, 'a battle' to defend against what they experience as an assault on the self. Student group life, relations with teachers — indeed, the whole teaching and learning process — encounters with administrative and bureaucratic — legal authorities, are all ongoing events that are shaped — on the students' side — by the tenuous character of self value and an approach to the world through the prism of a self-sensitivity born of fragility and uncertainty.

While there are career ambitions not unlike some of those at Grummitt High and college aspirations, including some specific ones, like at Penbroke, the drive to achieve rests within a more evident and pressing need for self affirmation — in the present, at school and in the future, by the attainment of 'safe' occupational positions and the indisputable power and certainty guarantee of money. Unlike students at the other schools, the Washington students' ambition is created under conditions of adversity not of their making and against the circumstances of neighborhood and, for many, also against obstacles put in their path by the school itself.

There is at Washington, what Crichlow (1991) refers to as 'the minority sub-culture of achievement'. In fact, it is institutionalized in the school in the WAETT program — Washingtonians Achieve Excellence Today and Tomorrow. The WAETT program is an academic club, with achievement entrance prerequisites and an emphasis on activities that will promote academic and career success. One of the things that is unusual about the program is the participation of volunteers, the 'Role Models' as they are called. Many of the 'models' work at The Company and come across town to share their own path to success as minority professionals. Mr. Green, a Company engineer, volunteers many hours helping students develop 'study habits', organizing community excursions to broaden their occupational horizons, and providing inspiration, for example, at a WAETT meeting.

Mr. Green: Anything else that you want to put on this year's agenda? Slides? Projects? Community activities? I am just throwing out ideas. I want you to take the INITIATIVE as a team — the Washington team. Our motto is to what? To take initiative and to be a strong example. Do you think you can do that? Do you think you can be an example for other WAETT teams? What things do you think you should be doing to show that you are strong academically and in society? Everyone can benefit from study techniques and so today we are going to introduce some of this as far as what is important about studying and how to study effectively and that is going to be the second part of the program that we want to do. I am going to try to cover some of the key questions about why we need to learn and why we need to study some of the methods. . . . In the meantime, did everyone fill out one of the WAETT Commitment forms?
     I want to introduce you to a new Model, Miss Springer. Miss Springer is from The Company.

Miss Springer: I am a chemical engineer and I have worked at The Company for eleven years. What I do is . . . I hope alot of you will be interested in these scientific subjects.

At another WAETT meeting, the faculty advisor speaks to the students:

I have one big gripe for eleventh and twelfth graders. Alot of you have not been taking advantage of the SAT workshops to help you prepare for The Test, and we are back to the same thing. You say that you are interested in doing things to help yourself, but when opportunities are available for you, you do not take advantage of it and I have checked the scores. . . . Nobody on the team is scoring high enough to get into the college of their choice so you really need to go the sessions. . . .

Despite this somewhat ambivalent communication of excellence and likelihood of success, WAETT students see themselves as different from the rest of the student body.

Student: It's not the majority of the people that are smart or conduct themselves in an orderly manner, and since it's only the FEW OF US, or you know, a small percentage of WAETT students — we are supposed to conduct ourselves different from other students . . . only smart people get in that group, you know. I mean you have to be really bright, the cream of the crop. I feel like I have achieved certain goals in order for WAETT to accept me and if I had to stay in school a million years to qualify for WAETT, I would.

Second Student: So, I went to the program and learned alot. I learned something that, you know, it made me FEEL THAT I WAS SOMEBODY BIG. The WAETT people always make you *feel like you are somebody, doin' something*. . . .

Not all student ambition is centralized in the WAETT program. A sixteen-year-old student recounts how she was determined to succeed — return to school, get good grades and graduate from high school — despite the birth of her child. The road to high school, and then life achievement, is through 'struggle', a struggle undertaken with the support of family.

Student: I am going full speed ahead and am not going to look at nothing that I left behind. Whatever I left behind — leave it alone. I am not going to look back towards it. I am going to go towards the future where I can get things happening, get brand new things.

You have to got to struggle to get what you want. It goes for Blacks, Whites, Puerto Ricans — I don't care what color you are, Chinese and all. You have got to struggle to get where you are or unless you were blessed to walk out there and get a job. It is not easy for me to get a job . . . but I know that struggling is the best thing you can do if you are determined to get where you are at. I am not going to give up on one thing that I want or want to do or want to have. If I have got to struggle to make it anywhere, I am going to do it.

Warren: What is the nature of the struggle that you see these days. Why are so many people having to struggle?

Student: Because it is hard. There ain't that many jobs. There ain't that much money coming in and like The JOB program ain't giving out much money. I don't want to go on welfare. I don't want to take care of my son with welfare, I am able to work and to use my hands. I want to give my son the things by me making the money myself . . . I come to school for eight hours. It is just like a working job, but you know, you are not getting paid for it, but you are learning. . . .

Warren: You really pushed yourself alot.

Student: I know that is right. I sure have and I am proud of myself. Tell everybody that I struggled to get where I am at today. . . . My mother and older sister always talk to me. My older sister is smart even though she didn't finish school. She has two kids now and she is going to become an RN nurse. She goes full speed ahead. She tells me 'Don't let nobody hold you back . . . If you are going to go to school, go and go to the classes and make something of yourself.' They know that I can do it. They tell me don't worry about no baby sitter because you got family — somebody that loves your kid and is willing for you to go back to school. I am just proud of my people and I want them to be proud of me. That is why I am going full speed ahead. I am going to show them that I can do it.

'Getting over the system' — achieving in school and 'gaining respect' are 'what it's all about'. The most superficial interaction is an occasion for self affirmation or self deprecation. You can gain respect through academic achievement, by dressing, by dancing, by fighting. Your appearance is important: 'You can tell a person by how he acts, how he dresses, just his actions. You can tell somebody, you know'. Reputation reinforces your self value: 'One good thing about your reputation. When somebody walks by that guy and says, "Hey he is good. That is my guy. He is decent. He knows how to behave and everything". You feel good and keep spreading that and I think that it is good for your teachers to know that you are a decent guy. . . .'

Respect gained in school may be an indicator of future respect, a sign of potential. A member of one of the many dance groups in the school explains the future importance of his current recognition as one of the Star dance group:

> If we *gain respect* right now as The Stars, then when other people find out, they are going to say 'Hey, well if he has enough interest and respect from a Star, then he will have this interest and respect in being what he wants to be, a doctor or whatever'.

Self respect is, however, under assault. The student classification system — which is designed not only to facilitate instruction by having at least relatively homogeneous grouping, but is also necessary 'to classify' in order to get additional state funds by fitting 'special program' categories — is experienced by students as an organized process of self derogation. The school — 'the system' — presents itself as an educational authority, and is recognized as at least an educational gatekeeper — 'you've got to get an education'. But, for some, its educational authority and knowledge is really a front for its power to impose illegitimate moral judgment. One student talks about his classification into the growing number of 'special education' students at Washington High as a process of self-regulation. The regulatory process uses therapeutic and educational languages, in order to 'check up on me'. But, after three years in 'the program', the student concludes that what they're really doing is checking up on his moral orientation to the system.

Student: Well, what is its ... Now what they used to do, lookin' for me, you know. They used to see how you act and stuff like that. *Mostly, they just watch your attitude.*

The regulations of educational and therapeutic classification are experienced here as moral judgments which have the effect of losing respect, of assaulting the self and threatening the quest to become somebody. Your reputation is damaged by the system's stigma.

Student: Well, it's like they don't understand. They say well, Millard is cool. What's he doin' in that class? I can't say nothin. What can I say? Can't think right off. People seen me right out in the hallway, coming right out of this class. They say: 'Wow. He's in a special ed. class'. Now I see him in there every period. What am I supposed to say: 'No. I'm not in this class. They put me in here, but I'm not in here. You know what I'm sayin'?

The student talks about his re-classification out of special ed in terms of a self-emancipation.

Student: They came back, seventh period and told me that they recommended that I get out. And that was it. It's all free — no more checkin' up.
Warren: Checkin' up?
Student: No more tape. No more having to put out things about what class I'm goin' to. No more teachers followin' me and everything — tellin' me how I'm supposed to act and how I'm supposed to do and that to do . . . It's more like now I can do things on my own without somebody . . . they always have you under close watch . . . because when I was in there they used to be checkin' up on me. You know, I say: 'How you know I wasn't there'. He said: 'Because I was there and I check on you'. . . . When you're in special class, they always gonna have you under close watch. . . .

The student felt that the level of the class was inappropriate for him, and that he truly didn't belong in a classified, special ed class.

Being in a special ed class is like being back in the sixth grade. And you can imagine what it's like — the work. The work is like — the readin' is like fourth and fifth grade. You open up one of those little story books and Tom had this little dog and one day, and some junk, you know.

The student's account of how he came to be there:

That's because I was never told nothin'. I was never even informed of what I was doin' wrong, and they never gave me no help or nothin'. I tried to tell them, I tried to tell them, you know, I just have problems comin' to school. They never even tried to help or nothin. It was like well, 'He didn't come to school for seventeen days so we'll put him in a special ed class. He don't care'. And bam. They took me out of regular class . . . I was trippin' out, you know, I was wondering what was going on.

After a series of tests and interviews, the student was classified as 'emotionally handicapped'.

Student: They say I'm emotionally handicapped. I mean, you know how many people out there are emotionally handicapped in that hallway. I'll bet you, I'll bet you at least seventy five per cent of this school would be in that class that I was in.
Warren: But how do you define emotionally handicapped?
Student: Emotionally handicapped — Easy to get mad. You know, that's what they say. People that's easy to get mad. They don't listen to you . . . Well, how can you — you GOT TO GET MAD, you know, 'cause you want to know why you were in this class and why you have to do this work. You be sayin to yourself: 'There's nothin' wrong with me. There ain't nothin' wrong with me that I can see'.

Millard reflects further on the etiology of his classification:

And the people who put me there, they didn't even care 'cause I didn't see them. I don't know where they are, what they want. All I know while I was goin' through all this, they could be out playin' golf somewhere. They could be dead and gone and I'd never know. Every time I ask who was the people who put me in this program, you have any idea'? They got all my records, but nobody knows who put me here.

Millard was retested and notified that he'd been removed from the special ed class:

Millard: And then they sent me this letter that I'm de-handicapped.
Warren: It said 'de-handicapped'?
Millard: I'm outta that program . . . I'm gone.
Warren: Can you describe that feeling. You know, what was that feeling like when you were being tested?
Millard: It was like — feeling like — days they'll call you out the special ed class to go up to see the psychiatrist. You know, the stuff they ask you is really annoying, and you get mad about and they say: 'Don't get upset', you know; 'I'm just going to ask you a few questions'. They always try to calm us down. You know, by the time you leave, you're on your way back to class, right?
Warren: um humm

Millard:	Somethin' like go to fourth period, you be so upset you just don't feel like doin' nothin.' You just get mad. *You just feel like gettin' your coat 'n leave, you know?*
Warren:	It's like humiliating.
Millard:	Yeah, so I just used to leave and I didn't go to class . . .

Repeatedly, students express the need for self assertion, for an arena for self development, for pride in self, and some concrete embodiment of one's ability for self-determination that leads to self regard. The battle for the self takes place among students as well as between the student and the administration of the school. It is represented in the descriptions of the present and in expectations for the future. The young woman student who returned to school after having a baby tells the story of how she had to defend her self esteem by fighting another girl in the school and how important self respect is to her.

Pamela:	. . . then they made sure that she was out of the building and they really kicked her out because she had this bag of bottles that she was going to hit me with and try to knock me out. But after that she left and everything was OK. But right now today I see her and I was pregnant last year and she looked at me and rolled her eyes but I don't care because I can still walk with my head straight up in the air . . . I don't like nobody to try to get over on me or nothing. Anything that I have got is yours *as long as you respect me and are not disrespecting me* and then everything can be fine.

Insults and fighting are one instance of the struggle for self affirmation. The future also promises the possibilities for establishing yourself. You want to be able to show something real and concrete — self proven.

Student:	It is hard to get a job. You think of Blacks and you think of a stereotype — welfare and lower class, pimps, you know, general impression. I don't want it like that. I want to be able to standup and say that *I have got this on my own and this is mine* . . . I want to pull out a credit card and say, 'This is mine'.
Second Student:	Tell him Eddie. It is all about 'to get over'.
Philip:	To get over?
Student:	To get over the school, to get over the system, to get

	over the hump. It is just all about getting over. *If you can do it, you have got it made.* But you have to do all of those things between here and getting over.
Student:	There are ways and shortcuts.

Self Determination and Self Assertion — Becoming Somebody

Student: I just want to be able to do what I want to do . . . and have something that I like to do when I work. . . . Whatever I'm making of myself here — that's what I'll be out of here. . . . Something in business . . . I see money in that and maybe I'll get a contract with The Company. It's just one thought I have. You know, I don't want to have a big business or nothin' — *just something that's my own and that I'm in charge of* . . . 'Cause right now, you know, somebody tell you to do something, you don't always want to do it, but if it's your own business or something, *you can tell yourself what to do.* . . .

For some of the Washington students, the school represents the most immediate obstacle to achieving self respect. As 'field worker', I preface a question with a brief summary of what the study is about and the student's condensed response makes even the brief summary appear overly long.

Philip:	. . . So then, what is the story here.?
Student:	You have got it. What you see is what you get.
Philip:	So what do I see here?
Student:	Maybe somebody else could tell you better.
Philip:	Why is that?
Student:	Because we don't take it seriously. You have got to take it like that or you go crazy . . . the teachers don't treat us right . . . they make us seem like dopies.
Second Student:	Yeah. They don't treat us with any respect.
Third Student:	Oh, my teachers treat me good. I give them respect and they respect me.

One student, Henry, elaborates how his encounter with the school's administration becomes a process of defending self respect and how discipline becomes a method of self-derogation — a self-derogation beyond what he sees as warranted, a surplus self-derogation. After being brought to one of the assistant principals' offices for tardiness and 'backtalking' and fighting, Henry complained about the way he was treated.

Warren: But that is the assistant principal's job.

Henry: Yeah, but he got to holler at you like you are a dog? Do you know how it feels to get hollered at like a dog? A dog knows when you are hollering at him too much. He hollers at you like a dog. . . . He treats everybody cold-blooded. . . . I am going to try to kill him because I hate him. It is a battle, man. He is for himself and I am for myself too. That's how it is. . . . If someone wants to offer me a nice amount of money to blow down this school, I'll do it. I am not scared.

Warren: I am still trying to . . . I mean what do you want out of a school?

Henry: I just want to know somewhere I can go with nice teachers and everybody is friendly and having a nice time and where you can't be scared in the assistant principal's office . . . I want to be able to go in where he can tell me I'm suspended. Fine. Don't let it happen again. Fine. I know you had to defend yourself, it was self defense. BUT, if he is going to holler at me like a dog. . . .

Warren: So you are willing to take the consequences of the action but you just want people to . . .

Henry: . . . realize not to fuck over me.

Warren: You want people to give you those consequences with at least some semblance of self-respect, not treat you like . . .

Henry: like a dog. Like . . .

Later in his discussion, Henry explains to Warren his views of discipline in the job world, and Warren points out the apparent inconsistency with Henry's actions in school. Henry then explains the difference.

Henry: I mean your boss rules, you know. But to keep a job — my boss holler at me — I am going to take it because that is what you have to do to get the flack.

Warren: I don't understand. How come you would take from a boss hollering at you by you won't take from the school official hollering at you?

Henry: Because Mr. Walters, *he ain't givin' me nothin', understand?*

> *He ain't giving me nothin so I don't have to answer to him,*
> *understand?* You know the boss is not going to give you
> nice money if . . . but, Mr. Walters, he don't give me
> nothin' . . .

Warren: Henry, go to class. Don't be late.

Group Life

Warren Crichlow's (1991) analysis of Washington High emphasizes
the academic stratification among students, between 'those who try'
and 'those who don't'. He describes the students located in the
basement, literally and in academic terms and their difference from
students on the upper floors of the fort-like building with endlessly
long corridors. Those 'few of us' in the WAETT program and the
somewhat larger group of students taking courses which prepare them
to pass the State examination, the 'State Test', differentiate themselves
from other Washington students and achieve their recognition and
reputation by virtue of their academic affiliation.

Warren: What do people mean by 'State Test' student? I keep hearing that phrase, 'This is a State Test student'. . . . You described yourself as a State Test student.

Some of these students differentiate themselves by saying that aca-
demics, rather than any one of the alternative routes to self-validation
in the school, is their method of self confirmation.

Student: There's more to life than fights . . . there's learning.

Fighting is, however, a realistically salient part of group life at the
school, and academic success is the most invisible method for 'gaining
respect', despite its well acknowledged value for future career and
money attainments. 'Reputation' is the immediate fruit of successful
self work in the school; and that work is the work of self-establishment
in the channels of status competition. It is 'political' work, as a student
observes: 'That is the reputation . . . it is prestige. Everywhere you go,
no matter what you do, you are known — like politicians are known.
They are in the papers all the time. *School is just like politics*'.

The politics of reputation and status competition for the regard
that constitutes the fundamental ingredient of self value, is a *visible and
present politics*. It takes place in the most casual encounters, where a

kind of 'one upmanship' is the way that differential self value is estab-lished. The self is on the line in the establishment of status hierarchies, more transparently and in less mediated ways than in the identity politics of apparatus-mediated and compensatory identity establishment at Grummitt High, for example.

Pamela talks about the fight that she was involved in and how the verbal self/status dueling of 'drilling' led to a physical fight.

Pamela: Yeah, and she was talking about what she will do to you and do this and that and you wear something that looked funny and she didn't like it and she will *drill* you on that. I was the type that didn't go for it, Ok? An' I tell her, 'Let me tell you something, I am grown just like you and the only thing that you have got that I don't have is a baby'. She got upset. She said, 'What are you talking about my baby for?' ... (See, I was five months pregnant, but I didn't know) ... I didn't want to fight her. She wanted to drop me and everything and I wasn't going to run ...

Some fights start out of school, in the neighborhood, carried over from pre-high school days, or begin in Skateland, where Washington High students like to go on weekends.

Warren: So what goes on up at Skateland?
Student: A lot of fights.
Warren: But people are there to have fun, Why is everyone fighting and arguing?
Student: They get mad if somebody knocks them down by mistake and he said excuse me, but he knocked him down and looked back and then he won't say nothing, but he will shove him and then they will start fighting. Or more generally: There is always somebody out there that wants to mess with some-body all of the time.
Philip: Why is that?
Student: People think that they are better than other people. To me I know that there is always somebody better than some-body. I know that for a fact.

The fighting takes place in some of the school's neighborhoods.

Warren: What is it like along Paris Street where you live?
Student: The parents — most of the parents get in fights. Or

	the fights are from earlier times. I didn't like school number two hundred and thirty, where I went before. They were too wild . . . they was throwing stuff, fighting, beating up people.
Warren:	And then you came to Washington and got in a fight? What was that fight about?
Student:	. . . I was talking about his mother. . . .
Second Student:	Where I went before was not a good school. There was knife fighting, I was fighting in the sixth grade and somebody — a few kids be bringing guns, razors, and it is just not a good school. . . . so, in this fight, I was at the sink, washing my hands and I felt this brushing over my back that someone was coming and I turned around and it was her with a knife and the teacher couldn't do nothin'. It was like a minute — it was either me or her, so I just hit her.

There are many stories about fighting gangs, who appear to have come and gone from Washington High; their return is constantly rumored. 'They had t-shirts with names on their backs . . . and if you started with one of them, you'd know you'd have to deal with the other seventeen of them'. Neighborhood shopkeepers observe that students are afraid to go to school because they might be beaten up, and so they form fighting groups as a form of self-protection. But the main story of a self-protective fighting group formation is one of 'the brothers' gang, formed in self defense against an assault on them when they ventured into a white neighborhood.

Philip:	Who were these guys who jumped you?
Student:	I don't know. There were just a lot of guys, about fifteen or twenty.
Philip:	Because you erased the Klu Klux Klan writing on the wall?
Student:	They saw that we erased it so they say, 'Why did you do it' and we said 'Because we don't like it'. They say 'You are in the wrong part of town' and we say that we can go anywhere we want.
Second Student:	They try to say that only white people can go over there, near the zoo, but anybody can go where they want.
Philip:	Yes.

Student: So I said that and they pulled back and hit me in the nose and we all started fighting ... and then we started 'the brothers'.

Most fights are among friends, and their friends, who join the fray.

Student: Last year, I was teaching him how to dance. But this year, him and his friends had their OWN GROUP so he kept coming and bragging and messing with me. One time at skating, one Saturday, he was coming up to my face, talking alot of junk and when we came out of school he came up to my face talking stuff and so then I told him to *get out of my face,* He wouldn't ... the boy from the other group came up to my face and was still messing with me. So I pointed in his face and by mistake I hit him. He came and we started fighting and we got suspended for that day.

There are less extreme, combative forms of individual status competition, especially dressing and dancing.

Student: Yeah, most of them they just try to look decent, maybe some of them trying to look better than other people. They be trying to look all cool ... they don't want to go looking all sloppy ... You try to look good — better than other people.

Small groups, like the Stars, make their reputation by dancing, while others have joined the MiniAngels, a paramilitary, neighbohood self-protective organization.

Student: You see we always wear our colors like on a set day, like probably a Friday. If we go out, we wear the same colors. We have got a dress uniform. We have got two separate dress uniforms that we use. One like you run around patrolling. We have got another one that is our dress uniform — you go out in, clean shirts, baggy pants ...

Uniforms are also worn by the dance groups:

Student: It is like we be alike because we don't want to be going up on the stage looking different if we are going to be doing the same thing so we try to get the same kind of clothing.

> Like the suits. It really don't make no difference. As long as they are the same thing and look decent.

The groups try to avoid fighting, and to gain reputation wherever possible, peacefully.

I don't know. Like we're joking in the neigh-borhood. We talk about each other's mother and all that, we talk about getting high and all that and then coming down to girlfriends. It seems like they'll say 'your girlfriend' only jokingly, but they wouldn't talk about it seriously because *they might get offended or something*. Students want to 'be friendly'. Don't hang with the wrong crowd and try to be friendly with everyone . . . the main thing is to get along with other people. I think you can learn it — all you need is the effort to try. . . . I feel like fighting is for the ignorant . . .

Most friends are 'regular friends', people who know each other from pre-high school days, who walk to school together or ride the bus; people who live in the same neighborhood. People hang together by neighborhoods. The neighborhood is still an important basis of belonging for Washington students, although some long for a different neighborhood and a different life.

Student: Yeah, like the people on my street, Faith Street . . . they were apart, but they were close knit, you know. Like my father to the lady named Lois, down the street were friends. You know, like Lois she liked to play the numbers and all that and my father does too. So both of them play and he goes to the store for her or he'll send us to the store for her and Jean, she was kind of the same way and she'll cook on Sundays and we'll go down there and eat and my father will cook and they'll come and all that — it's kind of closeknit or whatever. The street is fun, you know, but now it's getting different since a lot of people are leaving and all that.

Not all neighborhood pictures are drawn so affectionately.

Warren: What's it like around there?
Student: Up in my neighborhood?
Warren: Yeah.
Student: Oh, you walk up the street and smell reefer — people drinking having a nice time — kids in the road playing football. Playing double-dutch football and then dodging fights and listening to music and dancing, partying, having fun. *It is a nice neighborhood. But, you see, I would like to be where another neighborhood is at, you know.*

Warren: What do you mean?

Student: Like you know, somewhere down by this school — like you see the nice white houses over there? Houses like you know where you can smell a nice bakery-food cooking you know. But it is an OK neighborhood, you know.

Students spend their time trying 'to get it over'. 'Nowadays, trying to get over on the system, that is what it is all about. Trying to get something over'. They do homework, sleep, work, and watch television — especially cable TV which has the latest New York dance styles.

Warren: Can you tell me a little bit about what students do with their time?

Student: After school? Let's see, myself, if I'm not working, or I'm not here, 'cause I get out at the end of the sixth period, and then go home, maybe eat, watch tv, most of the time, watch tv.

Warren: A lot of hours of tv?

Student: Yeah, lots of tube . . . like four hours continuous — just watching it, and now to the news and then skip the news and . . .

Warren: Why skip the news?

Student: I don't know. It's just a habit. Or arcade, games. Arcade on Rivers Street. Ever been there?

Group life is a source of fun, avoidance of boredom, vehicle for self-expression, self-protection and self-confirmation. When the neighborhood, the challenge of people who are trying to get over on you, the school's no-reward administrative discipline structure, or being in the academic basement (or worse, misplaced in the basement — 'Like I was sent in there to be an observer at State Prison or somethin'') provide no self-sustenance, there is a place beyond group life — 'in my own self', where the self is secured.

Student: Yeah. Like if I have got me a bag of reefers you know and I go to school, you know — I know if I have got me a bag of reefers in my pocket I know I ain't going to make it all of the way through school today. I'll make it all the way through, but you know, *I be kind of in my own world you know*. I kind of be in my OWN world (my own business, my own credit card, my own self).

'Teacher do something', I'll say 'Fuck that', you know. I wouldn't even mind what he is doing. I let him go ahead because I would be feeling alright myself, you know. I would be to it in a mind of myself, you know. I won't be doing any work. They send me to the office. I don't mind. The principal will suspend me. I didn't mind. I would be in a place in myself ...

Warren:　You just sort of tune the school out.

Student:　Yeah. School ain't even in my mind, like that you know. *I am in my own self.*

Mobility

The same student, the one who walks to school from Faith Street, would rather not just be in his own mind. He would rather have money and get away from Faith Street, to a street of nice white houses. School is the way to get off Faith Street, almost all the students acknowledge: 'She be telling her that she don't need school, but that is a lie. *You need all the education in the world*, that you can get ... that is why — excuse my language — that is why some Black people today are so dumb. I am saying the girls, the dudes, they are just dropping out of school and the girls just want to have babies and don't want to finish. What kind of education is that? ... I am going to go to seven classes a day because those seven teachers will give me my future. That is education'.

'I know that if I want to graduate and be successful in life that I have to do good in school', is the majority, not minority, sentiment at Washington High School. The student's main self and family impressed obligation is 'to try'.

Student:　　　　I think it comes from the family, you know, tryin', or just telling you that you can do better than this or that. ... Yeah. You can't put yourself down. You know, you gotta really gonna get out there and do it.

Second Student:　You get those 'You can do better, you can turn out better' speeches from your family. And then just push yourself and take in whatever ... you know reap the benefits and maybe then you live on that street with the *white houses and the white picket fences* ... I just want something different than Faith

Street. And alot of it is 'money' because I don't want to be rich, but I want to be well off. And I know if I try and don't make it, then I know I tried my best, but if I don't try and don't, make it, then I never know if I would have did it.

The armed forces is a popular route to get money and further education.

Warren:	What appeals to you about the Marines?
Student:	The money. I want to get some money and go to school.
Second Student:	I want to go in the Air Force, really go to college in the Air Force. but then I was thinkin' I might . . . but I want to get away from here. . . . If I join the National Guard, at least I have a check comin' in every month and if I liked it in the service, . . . I go on regular status . . . I probably will just go in the Army and when, after they send me the money and then my mother, I will just send it to her, you know and then when I'll keep it until after I get back and enroll out of the Army and stuff like that . . .

Students want to avoid being on welfare: 'I saw my mother on that and I have no intention of doin' that . . . If you make it then that's the end of being on welfare and you can get a college degree or something like that . . . I don't intend to live like that because it's very depressing and I know what my mother is goin' though now and I don't have any intentions whatsoever of goin' through that'.

Student:	Without school, you won't get a job or nothin'. You have got to get an education.
Second Student:	No. There ain't nothin more important than that. Whatever I go to do it can't be more important than going to college 'cause that is my goal — *to get out of here* — at least to make it to the back door of college, you know, at least to be able to try it. At least be a student after I saw what it was like. I want to at least make it to the back door.

Student after student recounts how their parents, siblings and friends encourage them to study, succeed in school, and go on to college or jobs. For a few, it's a direct question of money.: 'I want to graduate, keep money in my pocket. Enough money to get high when I want. After I graduate, I am going to the Army and the only reason that I am going is one — money'. For others, it is occupational success and security: 'And I always take the best person and use them as a role model like the people that's Models in the WAETT program'. Students grasp quite directly the relation between school success and career success, whether they talk about life achievement occupationally — for the 'safest' positions, or monetarily, through the medium of enlistment in the armed forces. Some students talk even more specifically about how life in school — not merely graduation — is related to life on the job, and training for their futures. 'You have to always be on time. Just like at work you have to be on time or you get docked or whatever. It's just like at school you have to be on time, really. It do count bein' on time . . . not being late to your classes. Because that's just like a job. There is a connection out there'.

Hope for the future is tempered — except for 'the few of us' — in the students' encounter with the school. Many teachers are seen as encouraging and helpful. Getting an education is valued. But the school, despite the best intentions of most teachers, unintentionally depresses aspirations of Washington High School students. Caught in an avalanche of poor attendance, skipping, tardiness, state-mandated testing for classification for funds, perceived parental indifference and perennial budget cuts, the schools' teachers and administrators fight the alienating effects of an interaction between the collectively fragile self and the system that tries to help students achieve by getting control of what appears to be an uncontrollable situation. In getting control — for the sake of the students as well as the teachers — the school becomes another cog in the wheel of student failure, disappointment and dropout. The search for order and control, for containment or 'keeping the lid on', as Crichlow (1991) puts it, trips the wire of self-fragility for the many who interpret the institutional effort as surplus self derogation — a needless insult and offence to their genuine efforts of 'tryin' to become somebody'.

The School

Teachers

Teachers at Washington want to do a good job. 'Everybody is trying their best to help these kids', according to a prominent teacher who describes herself as 'a product of the sixties'. Yet, there is agreement that as one of the proportionately small number of minority teachers puts it, 'morale is in the pits'. Teaching at Washington, while it offers some rewards, is a hard job:

Teacher: I see it as a difficult task — being a teacher in terms of working with students who are unmotivated to achieve. But perhaps I am not giving up on that, but it is just somewhere along the line I need to find whatever it is and then have the ability to really get them motivated and to achieve and try . . .

The difficulty and frustration of what a teacher describes as 'the failure syndrome' is not generally for want of trying.

Teachers here are very busy. There's not much free time at all, you know. You're busy. A lot of them get in early. They're down at the Xerox machine or the ditto machine, writing plans, calling parents, administrative duties and there isn't much time. You really have a tough time completing your job — correcting papers — alot of pressure. You have to 'tune into the positive' to overcome the temptation to give up in the face of the pressures, the workload, and the students' 'failure syndrome' of poor motivation, poor attendance, and poor achievement.

Nevertheless, some teachers find the students at Washington 'lively and spirited' and delight in the school's ethnic and cultural diversity:

In general, you know, it's a very exciting school — you can tell just by the type of students we have, you know, we have students from all over — a lot of those Turkish kids, Spanish kids, Black and White, Orientals. I think it's just great. And different styles of dress. You have the very conservative dressers, very super stylish and . . . I don't know how much work you've done in the suburban schools — they're like clones — everybody looks exactly alike. They all have Levis jeans, Nike sneakers, they all have the Farrah Fawcett hair and the boys all have their hair parted in the middle and blown back. I mean they look exactly alike — every one of them and they don't dare to be different. And here, there is not that problem at all. A student can wear anything he or she wants to and nobody would say anything . . . I think that's great.

Teachers are aware of the difference in group life, between Washington affinity-like small groups of regular friends and others who 'hang' and the suburban school ethos:

> I don't think the jocks are very strong here at all. Now you may have your students who have real academic interest. But, I think in class maybe they deal with each other. But it's not so cool to be real smart so you associate with the rest of the crew.

Despite the problems of the Washington students, there are other schools in All American City that are more difficult.

Teacher: After I got transferred here, I realized how close I was to a nervous breakdown in the other building, because it was so hard. You couldn't even walk on the stairs. You had to walk very close to the walls because people were spitting down at you. The aide I had used got eggs thrown at her all the time. Tires would be slashed in the parking lot . . . you're always unconsciously worried about everything. . . . Working at Washington requires what a teacher calls the 'survival spirit' and an ability to charge and recharge your own energy supplies, particularly since there is 'tension' between the administration and the teachers, and you can't rely on teacher room conversation to motivate you. In fact, the teachers' room is more than a place of respite. It is also a place where teachers pursue their hobbies, fantasy next vacations, and sideline businesses — that enable them to continue to do a job that requires 'dedication'.

'I would say, generally', observes a teacher of ten years tenure at the school, 'that . . . our teachers are excellent in this building. They're very dedicated to their students, with an extra mile to help their students'. This same teacher, Mr. Robinson, goes on to acknowledge how much self-starting is necessary for the realization of 'dedication', and further, how many teachers have gone past that point, to the place of 'burn out'.

Mr. Robinson: Tune into the positive with everything. Tune into . . . let that motivate you and sometimes, right, I — oh there are days, especially on Fridays, sometimes I feel really drained, but I just keep going. I realize there's so much facing these kids when they get out of here.

Yet, Mr. Robinson, who tunes into the positive and is dedicated, is not certain that he would recommend teaching to young people.

Mr. Robinson: He said that he was thinking of going into teaching and I was quite upfront with him. I told him that the person who goes into teaching today, into education, must be very, very committed. You know, I was fortunate in how I got into education, but I don't think a young person should follow my example because it's too risky and not only do you do yourself a disservice, but you do a disservice to the kids you work with . . . you have to really believe in what you're doing and you have to work at keeping that energy level up . . . you have to communicate and try to project an image. . . . There are many people who are teaching whose 'energy level' and 'commitment' is just not up to it.

Well, to be honest with you, there are a lot of people who are still teaching in the profession that are teaching kids and thinking years ago. And years ago is not today . . . uhm, a lot of people are in the profession — this is just a paycheck and when you approach it from that attitude, you don't put very much into it and you certainly don't get much out of it. When they wake up in the morning — I mean most of us find it hard to get up in the morning, but I would say when you're talking to someone who is burned out, they hate the thought of it, even after they get in the door; they hate the thought of being here. There's a general lack of enthusiasm in their presentation to the kids — the involvement with the kids would be very limited because they see things as being pointless. *They've given into* the negatives. Probably the most positive thing they see is their paycheck and they probably count the years till retirement.

Among both types of teachers — those who keep their energy and dedication up and those who are burned out — there is constant frustration in their efforts to 'help' and motivate students by working with their parents and by trying to make changes in the school that they believe would be educationally beneficial to their students. Teachers who recognize that the families of many students care very much about their children's academic achievement, still report the difficulties of working with the parents:

> You see, you really have to solve your own problems. You want to get a handle on a problem with students, often times, by the time you go that route, so to speak, through the deans and counselors and everything, it just takes so long because you're *inundated* with so many other concerns and students. And then again, it is difficult for the teacher also because, you know, teachers have five periods a day. It's hard for them to get to a phone to call the parents. And you can only get through to about thirty-five to forty percent of the parents. Their phones are non-existent or disconnected for some reason.
>
> People are moving; they're at work. There's a tremendous problem of contacting parents. . . . If you send a letter home, the student gets the mail first, and they destroy the mail.

This is from Mr. Fern, a teacher who has faith in the intentions of both students and their parents.

Mr. Fern: Yeah, I think basically the kids want an education . . . their parents are pushing them too, explaining how important education is. I really feel that the parents are aware that to get the important things in life you have to have an education . . . I think that they want to break the welfare cycle . . . You know, nobody will admit to being on welfare . . .

Mr. Fern knows full well that the 1980s are not the 1960s and wonders if and when that time — that 'very good time' — of 'idealism' will come again. 'One of the people in the department was saying the other day', he recounts, 'How long do you think we have to wait until we get our chance again?' I said, 'Give it five years'. He was a little more conservative; he said, 'I think it's going to be more like ten'.

There is a crackdown on public liberalism, in the halls policy of Washington, just as at Grummitt and Penbroke; but the restoration hit the welfare sector in the pocketbook first long before the professional middle class had to ask whether it could truly afford two hundred and forty two elective courses and 'flex' scheduling. Efforts to make change from within, led by teachers like Robinson and Fern are met with the reality that a student knows, 'these are hard times; the state's giving less money'. 'In the schools, we're threatened, *of course*, with the budget cuts and all the things that that implies'. The budgets that do remain are bottom-line oriented and programs are pressed to show immediate results in standardized state mandated test scores. Where the 'self' needs to be reassured, if not rebuilt, programs can only be defended by immediate achievement outputs. 'I was just discussing the Rule 1 program with the principal yesterday, and the concern seemed to be that if we can't show growth, then how do we defend the program'. Existing programs need to be 'rationally' legitimated, in rationalized, standardized performance, 'bottom-line terms' — terms that can be magically understood state-wise, media-wise, and, as the WAETT program indicates, increasingly during these times, business-wise.

New programs are another story, entirely. The young teacher who escaped from the 'worse' school to appreciate the diversity of Washington High School explains how she thinks she can 'help' kids, and also how the budget cuts in educational programs for the urban underclass had direct impact on her efforts:

> I wrote up this proposal this year to teach a kind of psychology course using reading skills — just teaching the kids about self-image. 'I can succeed and I can be successful' — that theme — for the whole year. And the principal agreed: 'Oh, that's a marvelous idea. I love your plans'. I wrote all this up and I gave her a copy. Wonderful, wonderful idea. However, there's no money. . . . there's never enough money in the budget.

Mr. Fern also understands the importance of the students' 'psychology' in their achievement and discussed ways to break into what he calls the 'failure syndrome' by expanding and redirecting the counseling program.

Mr. Fern: I think that if we had more personal counseling going on . . . on a regular, on-going basis . . . uh, we have such a tremendously high transient population of youngsters . . . do we have — and I'm not offering any answers — but do we have a sufficient number of counselors for the number of youngsters? Is the ratio correct? I think that the answer to that is fairly evident. . . . It comes back to the common de-nominator — the dollars.

'The Attack'

For many teachers, no school program can compensate for what they see as the family deprivation. While Mr. Robinson says that 'most of the parents are really hard working people', he also complains that the students 'don't get enough love and attention'. From their most im-mediate perceptions, student attendance is the most fundamental problem, and visits to parents in order to improve attendance often prove unsatisfying.

Warren:	Well, what in your view is the nature of the attend-ance problem?
Teacher:	Oh, it is a huge problem that has to be dealt with. If you ignore that, you get into other problems — vandalism, school thefts, assaults, everything. Every-thing goes downhill when you don't deal with it.
Second Teacher:	I was visiting homes where children had skipped — the chronic absences were fifty to a hundred days . . . you have a lot of kids who just give up . . . the at-tendance problem has many reasons . . . they don't see a future in staying in school. . . .

The home visits:

> You walk into homes in which you have different levels. You know we treat a parent who is dumb the same way we treat a parent who has a lot of intelligence. . . . We give them all the benefit of the doubt . . . You don't see any newspapers in the home. You don't see any books . . . we are dealing with people at the bottom of the socio-economic scale. But there is a whole gamut, a whole spectrum to it. People on welfare, people moving around . . . the kids are suffering from *educa-tional neglect*.

The well-intentioned response — the benefit of the doubt — is to try to bring the student back into school by increasing the level of control and surveillance, by activating the ancient bureaucratic-legal apparatus of educational control that was invented more than a century before to get rowdy and 'delinquent' children off the street. Over the years, this bureaucratic mechanism of control has become ever more cumbersome. During the Restoration, it was called into action again, but with no great evident effect. Here is a literal description of how the attendance aspect of the 'benefit of the doubt' control mechanism works — the 'soft' side of the rusting 'iron culture' that I referred to at the outset.

> By the time we get an *attendance pattern* (there are several different patterns), right, like we showed you here — you get a letter home, you get a couple of home visits. You have a conference here. By that time you are already talking probably a couple of months and now nothing comes out so you send it to central office. They work with it for a couple of weeks. If nothing is resolved, they send it to Family Court and the Family Division has a hundred and twenty days to work with it. Well, because there are so many and, of course, it takes time to deal with all of these, and then you have got to get the different functions with them, maybe getting an agency . . . so by the time *they are done dealing with it*, you have lost a school year. You have lost a whole school year.

There are forms and referrals to social and legal agencies. There are disparate views about the motivation, capacity and sincerity of the parents. But seasoned teachers — even dedicated teachers who keep their 'energy level up' — do sigh and suggest that the problem is simply 'their whole attitude toward the school'.

Teacher: Just can't get up or doesn't like first period. They could come in at third period and sign in. They would be late for third period. It is just their whole attitude toward the school.

What is the students' reply?

Dean: [one of five disciplinary officers at Washington] Off the record, Clark, why aren't you going to class?
Clark: I go.
Dean: Second marking period you were out twenty of a possible twenty five days in English, thirty one in reading, thirty five times in social studies, thirty times in science. You tell me you have been in class?
Clark: Yes.

Dean: Ok, let's add them up. You were out fifty per cent. Astonishing.
Clark: Since the system started about the doors and not letting us eat our lunch in the hallways, alot of people have been late to class.

The 'tightening up' which at Penbroke means enforcing a relatively relaxed halls policy, where 'swat teams' refers to the mild-mannered boat-moccasin-wearing principal and two assistant principals, signifies something quite different at Washington. Here the halls are monitored by professional sentries, former Washington students, athletic stars who now work as part-time basketball coaches in the community center, and reinforced by the deans and principals. They huddle in the morning, drawing up the daily battle plan of hall 'attacks'. The 'attacks' are when they all take their assigned stations and stop any student who is in the hallway a moment past the change of period signal. Any student so apprehended is sent to the auditorium, where they begin the referral and, eventually the suspension process. The new 'attack' policy closes off some corridors completely, and puts added time pressures on students to get to their classes. Literally, it is a 'speed-up'.

'Today', a sentry tells me, 'we're going to "blitz" them.' When the 'blitz' begins, an 'attack' that is not just sporadic, but occurs during every period after the third during the school day, you can hear the deans on their walkie talkie radios, trying to coordinate completely leveled hallways. 'Where are you now 65? Where are you now? I've lost you. Over'. 'They're in the back hallway. I'm on my way there now. Is there anybody over there who can reinforce me now. Over'. *'Back me up at exit three. I don't see any problem on the third floor, and sentry two is over there by exit one, so I think probably assistance will be needed'.*

Students define an attack: 'And if you are late to class and you ain't got no pass, they will take you to your dean and they will say that you are skipping. That is all. Then you get in more trouble . . . They start asking you why don't you go get a pass and if you say you don't want to, they say you will have to come back after school and you are going to get suspension because you are talking back to the teacher. They are like getting into your case'.

Time is the problem for students in the increasing regulation of movement at Washington:

Yeah and now they have changed it around so much. It used to be easier *to get to class*, but now the whole system is changed.

They have got closed corridors everywhere. They want the students to arrive at their classes on time, but it is so difficult. Going through the halls, going through so much traffic because at the doors, people get jammed together, especially during the lunch hour. *Instead of five minutes going to the class because of the jam we have just two minutes to go to our locker and go to class.*

The 'blitz' of attacks every period changes the students' ability to *get to class*. From the school's point of view, the perennial problem of attendance and the 'pattern' of tardiness for which bureaucratic solutions are months in coming, needs to be dealt with immediately — to get the students into their classes by better management and control of the large physical space of the building and its outside perimeter. From the students' point of view, the 'attack' is not simply a speed up or too ready an entrance into the cycle of trouble. Rather, it is a *blockage* of the effort to 'do right' and to go to class, and more, fundamentally, 'to make it'. The attack symbolized — in the most concrete physical way — how the school, despite its attitude of 'help' expressed by the teachers, operates to block literally and symbolically, the student's effort to succeed. The 'attack' is the quintessence of the assault on the self.

Philip: Who are these people?
Dean: They came from the auditorium. They just got caught in the attack.
Philip: What exactly is an attack?
Student: The teachers lock the door and you *can't get in without a pass*. Even if you have a pass, sometimes *they won't let you in*.

More than anything, the locked doors symbolize the reciprocal of what teachers complained of in the discussion of attendance. It represents their whole attitude to the school — here, it represents the whole attitude OF the school. In both cases, there are, as a teacher said, 'many reasons'.

Student: I like Washington High. I have been going here for five years (seventh and eighth grades are included in the building). I like the teachers, the school. I don't like all the new doors they are putting in.
Second Student: I can tell you what they are doing. They need to change the whole system around.

Philip:	What do you mean?
Second Student:	Do you know what is happening in this school?
Philip:	No. I don't.
Second Student:	They are putting too much doors and the people are making the school look more dirty because they are writing all over the doors. They don't control the . . . fire doors, over there, here, everywhere you go.
Third Student:	They are lockin' us up in that school.
Fourth Student:	They lockin' us up. Aren't they lockin' us up, man?

The closing of corridors, installation of new doors, the 'blitz' of constant 'attacks' increases the number of processed students, of entrees into the 'soft' iron or bureaucratic system that is already a year behind in processing and 'resolving' the most difficult cases. Immediately, it is a communication to students that contradicts the helpfulness many seek and find among their teachers. More than an inconvenience, it is the sign of a blockage to 'makin' it', to class and beyond. It is the organized assault on the self, which the school has unwittingly come to represent — just as the tardy 'pattern' student 'case' represents 'their whole attitude.'

Student:	Right, and there's a hall attack. They will slam the door right in your face and they seen you running to make it to class and you seen that they seen you and you are going to stop and walk the rest of the way to class because they think you are on your best making it and they done slam the door and you knock on the door and they are going to open it and tell you to get a pass. What kind of junk is that? *And like they see you on your way there, trying to make it and they go slam the door in your face . . .*

Flashpoint: Teaching and Learning

The ditto and copy room is the busiest place at Washington High; paper can't be refilled fast enough, and within the budget. One method of keeping order and control is to use the class time for silent assignments, with some introduction and some closing on the largely silent and individually spent class time. 'Let's get busy', is a common command. 'Here are your assignment sheets'. Of course, many teachers do interact with their students, directly, caringly and with an attitude of helpful dedication. Not all Washington students, carrying the assaulted self from the reefer house on Faith Street through the affront of the attack's requisite front door corridor closing into the classroom is attuned to receive the 'positive' messages of teachers. On the con-trary, the inadequacy and lack of self assurance provokes the sensation of rejection, or more accurately, the classroom as the flashpoint of either turn-off or, more painfully of *exposure of the students' vulnerability*.

Philip: It is not too cool for your friends to see that?
Student: In class — in front of everybody they will *embarrass you* in class.

Students are sensitive to 'not being liked' by the teachers and attribute their academic problems to the character of their relation with teachers — just as group life is understood as an ability to 'hang' and to 'be friendly' in order to get along.

Student: If you do a wrong thing, one wrong thing, like if you get a mistake on a paper, he calls you a name.
Second Student: He goes 'jackass' — stuff like that — at us kids.

But the biggest problem is the student's inability to find a way to communicate with her or his teachers about their difficulty in doing the class work.

Student: You will be in class and the teacher will just give you the books and *they expect you to know it*. They say do it and you have just got to do it. THEY DON'T HELP YOU OR NOTHIN' . . . You have got to read it by yourself. I don't see why we need teachers if they're going to do that.

The testing and classification system is a common point of inter-action between students and the 'school'. The testing is not seen as a helping, learning or 'growth' experience, as Mr. Fern would put it.

Student: No they didn't encourage nothing. All they did — all they did man was take tests on you.

The students' attribution of the teacher indifference to their needs is more often cited than their own inattention to classroom activities. One student recounts how she turns off in class, disconnects from the teachers attempt at dialogue and retreats — like the reefer smoking 'I am in my own self' student — into her own world.

Student: Well, sometimes it is boring. We have to listen to this, you know. It will be like falling asleep and you just have to sit there and you can't take notes, cause they told you they'd give you the notes, and it be like goin' out one ear, you know, just *like in a daze* ... just sitting there thinking different things ... not what she saying. ... they not really paying attention to her.

One method of capturing student attention is the classified program, which occupies the basement of the mighty school, a basement where regulation is greater, and where students want 'to go upstairs'. 'I just want to get the help and all of that and next year I can get some better grades and come up from down there — come upstairs'.

Upstairs, in WAETT program, study technique learning is bolstering attention and underlining the drive to achieve and succeed. 'Efficiency, the Model', Mr. Green, says, 'efficiency is getting the maximum learning and retention for the least expenditure. ... But the key thing is that you have to have some kind of motivation ...' It's not possible to be 'in a daze' while Mr. Green, the volunteer Model from the Company, is addressing the WAETT students. 'I am hearing only one voice. Speak up. What's wrong with you?' he asks in a style almost evangelically engaging the nuts and bolts study techniques and the necessary 'motivation'.

Mr. Green: So we really have to work on changing some of our attitudes, I think. OK? That's all the sermon for today. Now will you pass around the collection plate [laughing].

Students' complaint that 'the teacher didn't like me' is amplified by Millard's dramatic declaration: 'Yeah they all of them do the teachers *cold blooded*. They all do the teachers cold blooded cause the teachers do them cold blooded ...' The typical Washington student keeps on plugging, trying not to give up. For them, school is like a job without pay, as the young mother who returned to school explained. 'Doin' right means doing your job in school. 'Goin' to all my classes 'n doin' the work. Just keep on goin' down the line'.

Warren: 'Keep on goin' down the line. That's some way of putting it. It's almost like an assembly line ... you seem to refer to school as work'.

Student: 'Like at the end of the day it feels like I've done a whole day's work and I'm tired or you know, the day goes along and we just keep on workin' on stuff.'

Some teachers seem like people to students: 'He gets along with you and try to joke with you and show you where you went wrong and all that'. The key, a student reveals, is to be friendly with the teacher, like with 'regular friends' and then you will get along.

Student: Yea, but I got it with a lot of — not really a lot of teachers — some certain teachers you can go in and say hello and *they'll speak back to you*. And during the year, you know it makes you want to *try harder in class. Maybe to impress you or something.*

    The regulated self, built on the sands of a tenuous, fragile self, the self 'drillin' others to gain small bits of self-value by apparent invidious distinction — that self, for whom one classroom sign reads — 'I AM somebody' is not 'goin' down the line' easily. The pedagogic relation requires more than caring here, and more than bureaucratic certitude of 'attendance'. It requires instead an attention that can only be engaged with the promise of both long term and direct self-enhancement. 'Money', 'safe' job positions, 'bein'' known — a reputation, being one of 'the few of us', the 'white pickett fence' are all means toward the compensation that is necessary. Of course, well-meaning educational reformers have had a hardtime at Washington High School, despite their dedication and effort. For the compensation needed here goes beyond skills and motivation.

    It is the self itself that has been eroded, 'cutback' even further during the Restoration years when moral virtue came to mean the appearance of authority succeeding. Meanwhile, the social order and the economic future was built on electives at Penbroke and on budget rescissions that came down to make life more difficult for both teachers and students who inhabit the basement that no one wants to be in at Washington High School. Students want you, the readers of this account to know — 'we are not bad; we are good'.

Chapter 5

Society in Reverse:
Microdynamics of Social Destruction

Identity in History

My initial intention to describe identity as the subjective value produced in a system of symbolic production proved overly abstract — another reification. 'Symbolic production' became an aesthetic pleasure of the analyst, paid for by denying the everyday historical context in which the action of becoming somebody takes place.

It is possible to describe a symbolic economy of identity (Wexler, 1988). Social interaction can be interpreted as a system of production where the means of production are interchanges of signs and where identity is its systemic, although individual and naturally-appearing, product. In such a Marxist, semiotic symbolic interactionism, there is a polarization of 'classes' built upon exploitation; the jocks construct themselves on the backs of the alcovian radicals. Good kids and losers, preppies, intellectual and yarders, WAETT program participants and basement special ed/Rule One students are the classes which result from the antagonistic relations of symbolic interchanges in schools.

Class resources are constituted by: a trust that allows bodily movement rather than surveillance; an encouraging admiration that fuels achievement-oriented confidence as opposed to the self-doubt of those who do not master self control adequately to escape the 'other program', or even just to manage not being 'always behind the power curve'; the moral approval of establishment role models and decency or the reputational stigma of being 'bad'.

There is a polarization within each class. Class polarization and the 'individual' identities that finally occupy each class position are the outcome of symbolic economies that trade in such strange currencies as shoe styles, hairdoes, sweaters, leathers, activities, attitudes, aspirations and all imaginable instances of so-called 'cultural capital'. The

shaping of identities builds on the symbolic materials and peer associations brought from the family and neighborhood, but especially as
mediated by middle-school self representations. People change, but
not without changing the symbolic materials they use in their interactions, and not without modulation by the institutional apparatus.
Deans' offices, favored or hated teachers, extra-curricular coaches all
can amplify or dampen identity signals.

This 'economy', however much it is the symbolic material in which
internally class polarized identities are shaped and constructed, diverts
attention from what the close analyses of the schools reveal as a more
powerful social dynamic. In each school (or class), particular social-
historical conditions have led up to a process where identity is formed
within a broader and more salient social movement. This doesn't mean
that we have to remain at the level of historical specifics alone; there
is a structure to the movement.

I interpret the case analyses as showing that there is a general
process of social emptying and absence or lack at the social center that
occurs in each case school (class). What is absent, missed and experienced, by at least some of the participants, as lacking is different in each
case. Identity is being collaboratively constructed inside and around the
vortex of the central social dynamic of 'emptying'. It is social relations
itself that is being emptied, and identity processes are class specific
compensatory efforts made against and in the ambit of a central lack.

The production model of identity is a systems model (Touraine,
1989), even though it is streamlined by the superimposition of a Marxist
economic logic on a dynamic and interactive semiotic medium. It is
a model of 'fullness' and realization, itself a cultural artifact of a theoretical effort to resuscitate industrialism by borrowing language from
that society's future. But there is no simple 'leap' out of the iron
culture. Its infrastructure decays and is dismantled.

There are recognizable patterns of social destruction; and that is
what I think we have found in our search for the school-work relation
that we phrased first in terms of 'commitment and disaffection', and
then discovered the engine of that social field in a symbolic economy
of identity. It is, I think now, not a 'full' symbolic production system
which needs to be described; instead, the social processes that create
social emptiness and a compensatory sociality — out of which may
finally emerge the terms of a new social field, rather than a modern-
izing grafting of new terms onto the old model.

Postmodernism is an historic cultural movement that carries along
within it not only new forms of identity, but also new directions for
describing what emerges from the destruction of social relations.

Beyond the 'Macro' Moment

'The end of the social' that Baudrillard asserted (1988) was one of many formulations that indicated a macrosocial transformation. In literary theory, and its social applications, it was the sign which replaced the referent or discourse that took the place of its object. Post-industrialism meant new workplace relations (Zuboff, 1988), where the connection among symbols supplanted concrete labor and face-to-face interaction. Postmodernism meant, among many other things (Turner, 1990; Wexler, 1990), the end of grand narratives (Lyotard, 1984), which includes also the story of society and 'the social'. This epochal transformation was, however, described in grand, macro social and macro cultural terms.

What I find in the school case studies are conditioned patterns of social withdrawal which challenge the basic constituent elements of social relations, or 'the social'. Instead of grand theoretical challenges to the concept of society, social, or social relations, I have described specific *institutional processes* that reverse the constructive or 'socializing' (Touraine, 1989) establishment of society: instead, desocialization, or society in reverse. Historical modernity, and one of its languages, sociology, filled the social space formerly occupied by feudalism and the cultural space of an interpretive theological language. But, for all the talk of the decline and passing of industrialism and its culture, what that actually entails in each societal sector remains still relatively undescribed.

Here, we begin to see what it might mean in schools. If we want to extrapolate beyond the cases and beyond the school sector, then we may have some concrete examples of what critical theorists write about in general terms as 'the decline of the public sphere'. Still more broadly, we see: elements of the decomposition of social relations; how identities are formed under these conditions; and a glimmer of new dynamics that are part of the transition out of the social infrastructure of 'the iron culture' toward new, though by no means more 'progressive' or benign, postmodern social forms.

Society in Reverse

Elementary Forms of Social Destruction

The political history in which the schools are described is the Reagan restoration — cutbacks in funding public institutions and the reassertion of 'traditional values', particularly in defense of authorities. In each school, there are examples and effects of fiscal retrenchment and efforts to reassert authority. But, the differences among the schools are deeper than the fact that at Washington High cutbacks impair basic educational services, while at Penbroke, belt-tightening might mean limiting the number of electives. Penbroke's 'swat teams' are a far cry from the 'attack' forces at Washington or Grummit's methods for branding the radicals. The deeper differences are an emphasis on different aspects of social relations. The similarity begins with the 'sign' or direction of those aspects: they are all negations.

What is at stake is different in each case: the negation of different aspects of social relations. These practical, institutional processes of social negation represent a destruction or reversal of basic social elements, which, when taken together indicate a reversal of society or, even an 'end of the social'. Not a macro, epochal transformation of media against society, consumption rather than production, or informationalism replacing industry; but, a set of specific institutional social practices that are *practical deconstructions of the social*.

In the working class school, *interaction* breaks down. 'Nobody cares' is the result of a socially conditioned mutual withdrawal of emotion and identification by students and teachers. The conditions or 'origins' of the failure move out from the dyadic social relation to the school's history, social composition of teacher and student groups, to 'the restoration', and then to class life during this historical time. In a poststructuralist vein, it makes sense to see this failure of emotional, identifying mutual social relations as the lack or absence at the center of the school — analogically, the class — which crystallizes what we ordinarily think of as antecedent conditions and the identity work of the participants, that I interpret as compensatory for the central absence. The direction and character of identity formation follows, as a compensatory reaction to what is missing: reciprocal, caring, emotionally full, mutually identifying social interaction.

The alienation of the interactional center of social relations does not end with defensive, compensatory self-formation. In the struggle for selfhood, for 'becoming somebody', the sad surrender of a caring, listening other is accompanied by a readiness to create individual presence, existence, also by using the images that come to replace interaction as the means of identity formation. Mass culture and its images are only a resource in the compensatory identity process, and in its availability to replace interaction as the medium of self or identity construction.

In each school/class, a basic constituent aspect of social relations is being destroyed. In the working class, it is interaction. For the professional middle class, as we saw at Penbroke, it is no longer, as Horkheimer and Adorno wrote (1972) that everyone is belabored by the social whole or totality. Rather, they are belabored by the *absence* of the social whole. Here, it is *society* that is missing at the center of school/class social relations. For the urban 'underclass' of mostly African American and Hispanic youths at Washington, virtually pre-school moral stigma and inferiorization makes society's constituent antipode — the SELF — tenuous, and if not absent, then certainly under attack and acting to defend against an imminent absence. *Interaction*, *society* and *self* are basic elements of social relations that are differentially expressed, in each school/class; but not by their realization or fullness. Instead, it is the emptying and putative lack of these practices and their representations which appears to stand, lacking and absent at the center of what we may still call social life.

The emptying process is unintended and overdetermined in each case. The attenuation of dyadic interaction is a by-product of distrust created by the school administration, in harmony with its community, as it strives for order and respect. The direct effect, of course, is social selection, stratification and polarization of student peer groups. The resultant atmosphere is one of containment and suppression. The 'good kid' jocks are somewhat exempted, as they carry an invisible hall pass of trust that is not always obviously coded in the clothing semiotics of student class polarization. But, they too, while they find adult identification easier, report that beneath the veneer of the classic high school culture of athletics and fun, they have not had much fun in school for a very long time — since their childhood.

On top of this pushing out of the ingredients of a full social center of interaction as unintended by-product of the search for order and respect, there are additional sources or conditions that reinforce the process of emptying reciprocal, identifying, bonding, or 'socializing' social interaction. Grummitt teachers took one step up from their overwhelmingly working class origins, and they don't want to be reminded again, as professional adults now, how bad manners and unclean appearance that students display can threaten to throw them back socially below whence their parents had risen.

The mass cultural difference reinforces class cultural difference, and gives a reason for a social distance opened up by fear, frustration, and a displacement of the teachers' own professional insecurity and threat from administrative surveillance, control, disrespect and uncertain employment. Family differences are part of the attribution of historically and culturally newly produced deficits among students. It is easier to forgive one's own ritualistic self-distancing from the critical interaction induced by organizational and professional dynamics of failure and frustration if the interaction partner is in a state of decline that takes them beyond the bounds where reciprocity can rightfully be expected: they don't deserve it.

The emptying of society is less perceptible, and can occur without projecting blame. You know, of course, as a teacher and as a student, that your personal self definition and ambition is nestled within your peer associations. Penbroke student stories of the pressures of parents and THEIR peers' ambitions show an articulated understanding of the social shaping of individual identities. Teachers may even acknowledge that their own professionalism causes a certain degree of socially divisive departmentalization. Students may complain about the 'apathy' and lack of school spirit.

Yet, these understandings appear as qualifications, addenda to the personal and professional self-centeredness, the struggle for an identity built only within a limited range of acceptable personal achievements, that ultimately pushes society out of the center of school/ class — only then to complain about the corrosive effects of its absence. Here too, parental family instability or overambition for their children can be seen as interferring with the school's order. But it is the order of individual performance outcomes, and not a sense of collectivity, wholeness, or society that is worried over. Only the non-instrumental violence, the school's defacement that can be easily repaired out of the administration's 'vandalism fund', gives a true hint of arousal and passion against a social center that, like the corporate executive style principal's ghost-like presence, is effectively absent. Violence against the null totality is the most visible acknowledgment that there is a school, as a totality, as a society.

At Washington, students fight against the institutionalized process of emptying, because their selves are openly at stake. Emptying here is of the self, and it occurs less behind the backs of the students than against their will, imposed forcibly and out of fear by their teachers and guards. The quest for control, unlike at Grummitt, is not so much to restore respect for authorities. Rather, it is the control of population management, an apparently logistical problem that presents itself as an issue of attendance. To the teachers for whom 'morale is in the pits', injuries to student selfhood are consequences of their need to manage students, individually and collectively, that will rescue them from having to face the pedagogically onerous task of overcoming students' many earlier deprivations or their own fears of students' violent uncontrollability. Dittoed in-class quiet assignments avoid the pedagogical encounter, while 'attacks' mounted by deans and guards usually prevent any unmanageable forms of collective self expression.

The 'committed' teachers can't free time or money from 'the system' to foster the sort of educational work that they know is needed to heal the socially inflicted bruised identities of their students. Selfhood is acceptable within the WAETT program, following the role models' Company career lines, but too exuberant an expression of local community forms is rarely applauded, as a young teacher did, for its cultural pluralism and difference of style. Instead, it presents problems for population management and gives cues of fear-inspiring uncontrollability when students are overly self-expressive outside the decaying forms of the old bureaucratic fortress of school. This vibrant self is not harnessed and elevated, but pressed into corners and locked out by the steel doors of school time.

Where the internal apparatus of control fails, the therapeutic and legal ministries reach beyond the school to 'the district' and then to the city's welfare management system. Self affirmation is almost always against the grain of school. Whether in moral or therapeutic language, stereotype and stigma are the interpersonal means of self suppression. The cognitive self gets in the way of the copying machine's lesson plan for classroom quiet, and the socio-emotional self challenges the bureaucratic control apparatus with its cultural vitality, just as it has for generations in the rational-legal system's solution to social order by self effacement. Washington has been an alien fortress in 'the neighborhood' for years. Now, it is only tightening the screws on self out of increased fear that 'the lid can't be kept on' collective self-expression for much longer.

Paradigm

'Society in reverse' enters the social scene after it has peaked or been made full by what the modern sociological paradigm called institutionalization and socialization. Any talk of 'decline' offends the modern sensibility's preoccupation with evolutionary progress and accumulative, expansive construction (Touraine, 1989). It really doesn't matter, however, whether the school/class was ever full(ly) institutionalized and socialized. We still observe a process that can be described from the inside, by participants, and from a more distanced interpretation, as withdrawal, and then absence. Emptying rather than fulfillment appears as the main dynamic underlying the different institutional processes.

Confounding the modern, Western view, absence and even experienced lack at the center (the realization or fulfillment of the emptying process) is not death and stasis. Rather, it is an uneasy motive, not one that presses directly for fulfillment by its complement or antithesis (as versions of dialectical sociology would have it). In our cases, absence is not a vacuum that is filled up, but a lack that is covered over, or turned away from. That sort of 'response' to the absence of key constituent elements of social relations is what I refer to, following psychodynamic language, as 'compensations'. They are compensations because, I believe, the lack is experienced by the subjects who themselves seek balance, but under conditions in which neither the center nor its opposite is fully accessible to help provide necessary structuration to self-formative, institutional processes of identity.

I see these school/class specific compensations as complex, including disparate, and even contradictory elements. In each case, one element appears paramount, but the minor chords are not eliminated. From within the compensatory formation of identity under conditions of centrally lacking sociality (interaction, society, self), there emerge 'foreshadowings' of what seem to be new and different loci of what may come to supplant social relations.

The sense-making interpretation of student and teacher lives within the schools does display a paradigmatic alternative, which includes: emptying, or, more concretely, withdrawal, and resultant central lacks in social relation; compensatory responses or adaptations in which identities are formed, that cover up or deflect from the lack; and foreshadowing, emergent elements contained within the compensatory process, that signal new relational forms.

To the analyst/composer, the interpretation is, of course, already in the case descriptions. By setting out these abstract elements, one hopes to reach beyond the cases to offer a more generally useful paradigm, at least for these historical times. In describing the cases, I have stayed closer to the participants' utterances and actions than I warned, composer-like, at the outset. Now, I do take analytical license, first, in suggesting that there is a differentiated, but similar structural movement underlying the cases, and that when those differences are recomposed, they are a recognizable, social narrative: institutional processes of identity formation under conditions of the destruction, emptying or absence of the basic elements of social relations.

Second, I extrapolate and ask that you imagine each of these schools as offering systematic insight, but not representative reproduciblity, into other schools. Further, I conjoin school/class to suggest that these class-differentiated schools be taken as exemplars or paradigms of key issues and processes beyond school, in the wider collective life of the class or social segment. Of course, that is an hypothesis, and studies of family, work, religious and political institutional life among different social segments is the only way to know whether to give credence to an ambitious analytical extension made here that school life is a lens through which to see wider social class life.

In my view, school IS society, and the so-called 'education crisis' is really the leading edge of a much larger crisis of public and institutional life. From that extrapolated vantagepoint, what we are offering is a microanalysis of an historical instance of social decline and destruction, seen from inside exemplary cases of a particularly salient institutional sector: education.

Emotion, Performance, Morality

Lack, compensation and foreshadowings refer to a common dynamic structure, across the schools. Analytic extensions can also be applied to the differences among the schools. What have been called the working class, professional middle class and urban under-class schools present different central lacks: interaction, society, and self respectively. Social analysts are accustomed to accepting that these pithy neat concepts are extractions from empirically mixed cases. There are absences (and presences) of all in each school. It is simply that one element predominates, to the point of serving as a typification of the entire case.

Just as a deeper analytical level can be identified that reconstructs the common dynamic structure, so too, I can suggest a deeper analytical level for the differences. A microscopic look at the interaction lack of Grummitt shows how much emotional needs and failings are at the core of the 'likewise principle' of mutual withdrawal from social interaction. Similarly, at Penbroke, the calibrating social/self process of 'getting psyched up', or, more often 'getting psyched down' is one of a plethora of clues that in deed as well as word, the professional middle-class' unintended evisceration of collectivity or society ('the very idea of the school') all turns on issues of performance.

At Washington, from the first student interview to the last teacher or administrator rationale, we know that the battle for the self is primarily fought in the moral domain. It is your 'attitude' that is being watched. While 'chilling out' may play a role analogous to 'getting psyched down', 'drillin', not 'getting messed with', and finally, 'becoming somebody' means self-affirmation in the moral order; as surely as the popular judgment that the school is 'bad' is more about moral validity than either performance or emotional engagement.

These analytic dimensions can operate as reductions, without the details of each case. With the cases, they are extensions, that invite us to think about what is at stake in each school/class, and about what precisely is being emptied for whom, and compensated with by what. The issues of working class life are more inclusive than the question of caring interaction, and to think that there is no moral element in the professional middle class or performative emphasis in the urban underclass is wrong and misleading. But, there are differences of emphasis, and what is most salient in everyday lifetalk, especially when it is missing, can have the greatest effectivity.

Gender, Class, Race

Although I underline social class as the main frame for coding school differences, within those classes there are further differences which highlight the differential importance of broader isssues of race, class and gender *within* the schools/classes. Across the schools, without suggesting that working class (school) life is mainly about gender, the major compensation to the lack of caring interaction is the formation of exaggerated or stereotyped gender differences. The Harley-Davidson leathers and Charlies Angels Farrah Fawcett hairstyles are signs of more general sex seggregated behavioral differences, which, I believe, are part of a process of identity formed within a lack of interaction.

Not only the early training ('they pushed Sesame Street on us') and compulsion to perform, but the achievement-locus of external cues for self-calibration that leads to a 'success without society' on one side, and on the other, a survival-wise, even pre-emptive suppression of expectations that carries over to a broader depression, shows how mobility and class dynamics are professional middle class compensations (as well as more obvious socialization continuations or 'causes') for the absence of collectivity.

At Washington, the pre-school basis of moral inferiorization is racial prejudice and stereotype. That is what students have really most to 'get over', to prove, that 'we are good, not bad', and that 'I am somebody'. The moral dimension carries no intrinsic connection to race; but, empirically, they are joined for the urban underclass, as both a precondition and compensatory response (recall how 'the brothers'

117

gang was formed to protect against future assaults) to efforts to empty selfhood, even unintentionally, by the bureaucratic means of surveillance and population management.

Interaction, society, and self are the lacking central elements of social relations. Emptying, compensation, and foreshadowing are the common elements of the dynamic structuring or process of institutionalized microsocial destruction. Emotion, performance and morality are the main constitutive dimensions of action underlying the institutional processes. Gender, class and race are ways to understand class differentiated compensatory defenses against the absence of basic elements of social relations.

Interaction

The disappearance of interaction is an ironic effect of how deeply needed are its rewards. 'My girlfriend, my parents' is an unusually open moment of admission of the hunger not simply for social contact but for secure dependence — for love. The working class suitor is rejected by another active voice, itself a part of the working class. The disrespectful chaos of liberalism heightens desire for order under authority. If the teachers, some of whom are feared to be (like hypocritical parents) 'flower children in three piece suits', cannot command order, then an added apparatus, a structure of discipline must be created to ensure the behaviorial analogue of neatness and cleanliness — the individualized bulwark against chaos from below, just as liberalism represents chaos from above, in the social hierarchy.

The discipline structure, as a bureaucratized substitute for patriarchal authority, goes beyond its early success in restoring order. It brands, punishes and pushes to dropping out all those who are not neat, clean and orderly enough in their behavior. The hurt of rejection by patriarchal authority, even in its bureaucratic guise, is the motive for setting up counter-identities which any semiotic would argue are plainly defensive in character. Identity if not formed, then at least consolidated in school, is drawn in self defense: a self defending self.

This hurt is not complete. Obviously, jocks, despite their premature earnestness, are not hurt in the same way. But, the jocks at Grummitt are likely to come more from either the rural parts of the school district or more 'middle-class' families. For a few, even in high school, athletics is already a channel of social mobility. But, for many, particularly the radicals and a vast intermediate group of 'nobodies' ('the silent majority?') identity is almost evidently built on the ashes of their rejection, which itself then becomes a fuel for solidifying their peer self-validation through like-minded associations and unmistakeable actions of defiance. Dropping out is only the last stop on a long ride. In encounters with Bech, who is simply the apparatus' agent, the hurt of patriarchal rejection is well hidden beneath one's leathers or spiked shoes. But, in Dr. Lyborg's besieged Help program, the hunger for positive identification within a history of experienced rejection is the most common story.

Even short of love and identification, attention and the listening ear of an adult other seems to be generally absent, outside of the Help program. In the competition for local power and funds, Dr. Lyborg's program, with its maternal-like nurturance, its cookies, sugar, sharing and openness is easily defeated by established routines of bureaucratic punishment, under the aegis of the 'bad cop/father'. The 'good cop/ father', back slapping Joe Kingman, knows how to bring kids around; they like him. But, the organization which he administers bifurcates love and discipline at opposite ends of the long corridor in iconic characters who disdain each other.

The rejecting bureaucratic authority has hidden helpers. The teachers, many just one step up from their recent working class origins, themselves frustrated daily not only by their students, but by a systematic lack of appreciation and recognition of their desire to do more and to fight the dangers of ritualized burn-out with professional autonomy, are the internal class actors, casting out their own 'fears of falling' back to the class stereotypes of socially rude and unacceptible behaviors and appearances. To some extent, the working class, in its division of character and labor, between teachers and students, for example, is rejecting itself.

Rejection in the name of control insures that the desire for love, dependence, identification and listening cannot find direct connection with most adult teachers. The bureaucratization of rejection insures that feeling will be mediated by a large field of signals, attachment to which at once substitutes for identifying love and full, even intimate, interaction. The apparatus' signs become the replacement for a positive interaction, that we have thought has historically served as the basis of the social bond. Instead of interaction, there is image. That is what I meant by summarizing peer life as 'alienated' identity formation. The class-based emotional dynamics of the school prevent interaction. What is so surprising is how prevalent still is the conscious, articulated expression of people's experienced lack of interaction of a more direct sort. Grummitt's real icon, its logo, is not its athletic teams or theatrical performances, or even the visible alcovian descendants of a vaguely remembered earlier cohort of 'radicals.' It is simply the phrase on so many lips: 'nobody cares'.

The 'end of interaction' takes place in front of everybody's eyes. The 'likewise principle' is the subjects' formulation of dynamics of interpersonal emptying and social withdrawal. Of course, the process spirals, the apparatus becomes more natural-seeming, and the withdrawal of the less powerful students is coded as an individual matter, a failure of 'motivation', if not ability, which can, in modern sociologized thought then be attributed to family failures. The dynamic through which social relations are emptied of interaction gets covered over by these sociologistic and individualistic attributions, false dichotomies, which, like the polarization of love and discipline, are part of the process of emptying social relations. But the dynamics underlying the emptying, the immediate and structural sources of interaction's attenuation, are too close to home to be ordinarily articulated. That happens in the rare moments of self-permitted vulnerability, and in the outside analyst's willingness to act as composer of a narrative in which bureaucratic discipline and consequent alienated identity formation are fueled by rejection and a lack of love. The effort to cover and compensate for that is the medium, the non-caring, anti-interactional space in which working class school identity is constructed.

Society

Penbroke is different from most 'all-American' high schools, even though it is in All-American City. Teachers who have been around know that lack of involvement in activities that represent the school as a whole is unusual. When activity happens, it is because the 'winning' is so notable and not because the team is playing. Of course, there are homecoming and intramural competition sorts of regular high school rituals. But, as with the 'winning', it is the extraordinary achievement, the almost 'professional' level of student accomplishment that stands out.

Students complain about the lack of 'school spirit' and the apathy. But, the complaint is half-hearted, a self-irony, a shrugging acknowledgment that subtly admits that the real action is in individual academic achievement. The 'intellectuals' disapprove of the conformist preppie dressers and are skeptical about the college rat race. In the end, however, they are caught in the race and envy the less visible minds who have garnered admission to a coveted college, who have entered the golden circle for which high school is really just a preface.

The students are indeed ironic, and even self-critical. They mock themselves for their lack of social conscience. Even as they do that, however, it is within a competitive comparison with their parents' generation.

From social activism to the price of home mortgages, they worry that they will not do as well as their parents want them to, nor as well as their parents have done. Even high achievers, in a self defensive casualness that irony helps underline, worry that they are not as good as someone else. Despite an impressive articulateness, it is only on rare occasions that one can admit to 'being behind the power curve' or 'loaded down' or even to being anxious and depressed. Instead, there is a tone of lightness, the casual coverup that works as a continuous 'getting psyched down' or 'mellowed'.

Emphasis on individual achievement doesn't mean that they don't have a 'social life'. They go to parties, drive around with their friends, drink, smoke, and despite their reputation for having high priced drugs, do drugs to a lesser extent. Sociability is, however, self-centered and recreational. They 'let off steam', the steam of grade achievement, in peer society. The school, for all its flexibility, belongs to what they call the administration, those inferior adults who fail to appreciate students' need for even greater personal freedom. Teachers are often respected, as purveyors of knowledge and skill. But, they are not much use in learning how to live, when students admit that is something worth knowing. Instrinsic regard for knowledge is not lacking. It is simply overshadowed by 'the pressure' — future oriented achievement that consumes attention, induces adaptive mechanisms of adjusting achievement expectations, and casts a pall of depressive anxiety over everyday life.

It is 'the idea' of the school, of a non-instrumental, non-status related goal, that fails to have a grounded, everyday meaning in students' lives. 'School spirit is nothing', is shorthand for the failure of the school as a whole, a graspable social totality, to engage energies that, while not completely dispersed in the separate compartments of individual achievement activities and worries, become increasingly irrelevant, if not hateful, as one approaches the golden circle of college acceptance and future elite social position. Some are not sure 'what we have missed'.

They are right to pre-empt criticism by admitting their snobbiness, condescension and disregard, because acknowledgment of their own 'apathy' is not just half-hearted. It is a boast, an accomplished non-engagement with all claims that are neither of instrumental performance value or are recreational breaks in the chain of achievement.

Students are then, ambivalent about how deeply to explore the absence of society ('spirit', 'idea', the school as a whole), and how seriously to estimate its impact on their lives. They really are not sure about what is missing. Not everybody at Penbroke is on the fast track of success. 'Yarders' can tell you what a boring place it is, how kids are consumed out of the present, and how they count the days until their forced proximity to success ends.

'Society' has come to be perceived as source of 'the pressure', and failure to identify with the totality is more than selfishness or busyness. Non-identification with the social whole of the school, where the totality is the origin of the pressure carried by parents, parents' friends, elder siblings, friends, and your own worst, self-punitive enemy, yourself (underachievement is 'the worst sin'), is another smart move in a self-protective game of hedging your bets. Achievement goals are what most immediately represent the larger society to the students. In the face of the competitive success market, they practice how to remain calm, even indifferent, as a protection against the injuries caused by failure in a success race that never seems to end. What is learned are strategies for managing infinite expectations, and, as a by-product, the formation of self as a process of environmental calibration control.

They are good at talk. Our researchers were stunned by the articulate apparent self-reflexivity among students. But talk hides the fear — of failing, of not fitting in, of not pleasing their parents (and even the teachers whom they caricature). Beyond 'the time pressure', and the 'loaded schedules' that they take as a learning challenge for their futures, fear is the reason that they cannot get past ironic boasting or nostalgic complaints about the school/society that is missing.

Identification with the social whole requires commitment in excess of rationally calculable return. What hegemony of the achievement market really teaches is not simply a highly individualistic or privatized self-centeredness, but a mode of relating that calibrates social investments in order not to be overly burned by wrong expectation levels. Identification with the totality is open-ended, and cannot be turned off and on with the speed necessary for emotional and self-esteem equilibrium. Society has already had its impact, through the achievement maze, and its attendant modes of adaptation — getting psyched up and psyched down. Like the disciplinary apparatus at Grummitt that comes on the scene to effect control and stays to provide a permanent mechanism of alienated identity formation, here too, achievement, society's product, stands between self and society, blocking direct attachment to something larger than its own sign of individual achievement. If the working class defeats itself, through a complex internal division, the professional middle class, despite its articulated potential power of consciousness, defeats and diminishes the capacity to identify with, to say nothing of lead, society as a whole.

At Penbroke, there is a tension between the teachers' pleasure of being part of the student's high achievements (and their parents high status) and their independent pride of professionalism. Their professionalism, (like the internalized students' achievement pressure, separates), in 'departmentalization', rather than unifies them. Like the students, it is talk, which for teachers is put more professionally as 'communication', that covers and compensates for deeper and more direct bonding with each other in the commonality of either their professionalism or membership in the same school.

The 'ghost-like', 'missing' principal is not the jovial, temper-raging father who presides over the institutionalized separation of love and discipline or even therapy and bureaucracy, that is Joe Kingman. Dr. Snowbridge is a 'phantom'. He makes up for his symbolic absence — no leaderly reminder of the social whole — with the same ironic lightness as students cover their fear of social commitment ('he tells a nice joke') and by resort to a remote control that appeals to teachers' everyday rhetorical method of only half seeking supra-departmental connections — meetings and more rationalized, professionalized forms of talk. Instead of a supra-department, school-wide totality, represented either by the principal's presence or a sense of teachers' common membership that transcends identification with excellent student achievement and interferring, but still valued, high parental status, expert-guided meetings that teach communication skills are what is left of the school as a whole.

Students, teachers and principal share awareness that something is missing (Dr. Snowbridge resigned shortly after this study was completed. He was replaced by a department chair admired for his casual style and communicative competence). There is a quest for more time in 'the Public' by students, a nostalgia for a cross-specialization place where teachers ate together, and an ironic, casual admission that 'apathy' or 'departmentalization' or a corporate-style, remote leader, leaves out, takes away, or, as I have said, 'empties' something central in everyday school life. In the curriculum, very few teachers question the wisdom of so many choices of 'flexes' or elective subjects. They wonder about the integration of knowledge, and, like the students' moment of doubt, whether education shouldn't have a greater emphasis on learning how to live rather than mastering the accumulation of grade and college-relevant flexibly organized fragments.

Success competition, professionalism, and specialization are the ready to hand culprits who empty Penbroke of its 'school spirit', its social oversoul, or, behaviorally, commitment to the social whole. The 'nothing' that replaces society, however, is reached more fundamentally by a fear of failure which leads to always hedging your bets and relying on the professional authority of one's knowledge and scientized interpersonal communication, rather than taking the leap of commitment that cannot be easily hedged toward a less easily managed identification with the social totality, with 'society.' Cool communication is the cover up for a society that may have overheated and over individualized its driving force of performance achievement.

The emptying of society is a cooling down of surplus success in the internalization or 'socialization' ('oversocialization' was not a theoretical misconception of functional sociology; but a middle-class naturalizing generalization of insightful self understanding) of its performance principle. The intensity of the drive and its reduction to highly individualized embodiments (so-called 'achievement') induces fear. The fear that investments can't be hedged or that boundaries can't be maintained is the professional middle-class version of the working class' fear of chaos. Here it is not some unruly other who will intrude, but the self/environment relation that threatens to overheat to unmanageable proportions. The emptying of society is a defense against the success which it has achieved — a dangerously uncalibrated compensation, by which the 'fullest' social class empties its societal context.

Self

Unlike Grummitt's extrusive branding of its radicals in the disciplinary apparatus of individual rule infractions, the control effort at Washington is collective and categorical. What stands out here is the difference between middle-aged women asking to see individual hall passes and former football players carrying two-way radios coordinating attacks to clear the halls of everyone during specified times. At Grummitt, students get detention, and at Penbroke, if they are deficient in 'self-control', they may be put in the 'other program'. At Washington, however, large numbers of students are systematically categorized as handicapped or incapacitated on cognitive, emotional or behavioral dimensions.

There is a highly rationalized educational/therapeutic apparatus for classifying students in various versions of special education, while what counts as immaturity at Penbroke or rebelliousness at Grummitt, opens the door to an elaborate legal apparatus for graduated disciplinary hearings, trials and expulsions. Washington's 'attacks' and its attendance mechanisms deal in a more categorical, systematic way with students that displays something beyond school 'discipline'. The school is engaged in the work of population management.

It is the 'whole attitude' of the student which is at issue, and not an ephemeral developmental stage. The conflict between the school's administration and most teachers and the students is not idiosyncratic or partial. It is categorical, systematic and based on assessments of the student's whole life trajectory — social origins, formal school classification and probable social destination. The school is not racist. A growing number of teachers and administrators are of African American or Hispanic American origin. Among the White majority of teachers, there are many student advocates and 'committed' teachers who are not burnt out. But, they generally accept popular sociologism, and see individuals in light of 'the failure syndrome' which is traced back largely to family deficits. Neither the family 'deficit', nor the school classification and dispersal systems, however, are pressed further to macrosocial questions of opportunity, class and race in All-American City (See Crichlow (1991) for an effort to make that connection to Washington High).

The students know that race is an issue, and even more, that the categorical conflict they have with the school is about more than specific academic performances or particular disciplinary infractions. It is about value, about morality, about 'good' and 'bad'. On the one side, moral value and moral disvaluation are not explicitly linked to race, though the students are clear that this is a minority school with mostly majority teachers and administrators. On the other side, the depth of the moral approval and opprobrium is unmistakeable. The self is on the line, and it is the self that is being questioned by all the measures that, from a school organizational view are a combination of committed uplift and population surveillance and control. The unspoken linked chain is race, moral value, and self.

Especially in the overcoming, in the multidimensional articulation of achievement ambitions — and always their direct connection to self-value — students reveal the ascribed racial character of their moral inferiorization and the depth of its penetration to the core of the self. That is why they have 'to get over' and, by their achievements, whether academically, occupationally, in appearance, style, dance, athletics, skating, and just plain everyday 'drillin' — interpersonal rhetorical skills of attack and defense of the self — prove that they are 'good, not bad' and that they 'shouldn't be messed with'. What they want everyone to know is not whether they are 'makin' bucks at the Company' or whether they 'got into Princeton', but that they *are* 'good not bad'. The social, educational categorical process, from its structural racial origins through its 'family deficits' to its school attacks, placements and proceedings, is an ontological process. The self is struggled for, to be filled up rather than calculatingly emptied or mellowed. Drugs don't let off steam from individual competition; they obliterate the categorical attack on the self, so that identity can be searched for in an inner, more secure space.

Social emptying of self, against which Washington students strive, modern-like, is an artifact of a set of macrostructural historical and socioeconomic processes that are finally enacted within the school organization as a dynamic of controlling and dampening self expression for purposes of population control. The population control, even the steel doors and anticipated metal detectors, may well be in the service of laudable and practical educational aims of 'getting the kids into school' and creating a more pacific climate for teaching. But instruction remains largely preoccupied with control, even as it moves away from the palpable force of the guards radioed attacks, and the therapeutic languages of classification and internal stratification to the copying room and the non-interactive, quietly controlled lessons.

Students are fighting, both with each other and with 'the system' to counteract organized attacks on the self. Fighting, of course, however immediately or generally self-defensive, is another occasion for system-processing, in which there is methodical forcible, legal, or therapeutic self assault. Along with fighting, a one-down self protects itself by intensified forms of affiliation and stylized self representation. Fashion like *The Gentleman's Quarterly* is a mighty effort to establish a reputation for decency. Status politics are so heavy because status is so vulnerable, from before, after and during school. Coming to school, if you are 'messed with' by the wrong people, can be a courageous act of self assertion. WAETT students, in the school's upper floors, are learning from the Company role models how to take tests and how to develop an attitude for success. They may fight less than other students, or even dance less, or dress less, but the same intense battle for stable selfhood is underway with the assumption that 'school is my life, my future'.

Self is struggled for in this compensatory defense, but it is also diffused. An intensified affiliation, the 'cuz bones kin' of really close friends and the 'reputation' won in the status politics of 'drillin' and 'not being messed with' makes carefully networked association a necessary element in the daily diet of self maintenance. The struggle for self activates powerful and expressive peer networks that decentralize the self, as the best, though ironically, self-defeating form of self defense.

Chapter 6

Becoming Somebody: The Class Self

Academic Field Setting

Attention to social microdynamics showed how much questions of identity or self are at the heart — even the absent heart — of social relations. Yet, new sociology of education, as Stephen Appel (1992) has persuasively shown, largely avoided these questions, or at best placed them under an amorphous umbrella called 'culture'. Perhaps, as Appel argues, there is a denial of depth psychology, or of all psychology, on ideological grounds. After all, new sociology of education flourished as an alternative to the bourgeois twins of functionalism and individualism, of system and idiosyncrasy. The sad effect is an absence of a social psychology in new sociology of education, and a failure to attend to socially patterned self-dynamics in school.

This effect contributes to the increasingly evident irrelevance of new sociology of education for understanding school life. What our studies show is how much in fact all of school life, for the students, centers around the daily project of establishing a social identity. Further, the microdynamics reveal the extent to which self processes are at the analytical core of social relations, albeit with a focus on their absent or missing elements. As the social relations and lacks are different for the different schools/classes, so too are the self processes.

The academic field horizon within and against which I write fails, despite its overcoded interest in 'class', to develop any textured understanding of class differences in schooling. Our finding is that 'becoming somebody', the identity project, and class difference, taken together, is what best makes sense of the social life of school. Even the postmodern slant on social relations — that it is central absences or lacks which are determinative — fits the more general view that school life can best be illuminated by a social psychology of classes. While I don't deny that I have some prior inclination toward such an approach (Wexler, 1983), I do think that the importance of a class psychology of the self emerged in the work of making sense of school social relations.

If radical, critical, and 'new' sociologists of education have failed, as an ideological-vocational hazard, to pay attention to self dynamics, the traditional wisdom of depth psychology has emphasized earlier childhood and family experiences rather than social institutional life as key for self formation. The effect here has been an underdevelopment of psychodynamic empirical studies of institutional life. Labier (1989) offers an important counter-example in his essay on worklife and emotional conflict. Critical theorists assume institutional processes are self formative; but they rarely study and describe such processes and their differential relations to self dynamics (Wexler, 1983).

Defensive self

My purpose here is not to provide a general theory of self or identity dynamics, or even to outline the dimensions of a psychology of social class; those are larger and longer range goals. I simply aim to elaborate and extend our observations on how an emptying of social relations that leaves different central absences in each school — absences that structure school life — affect self dynamics.

The process of self formation as compensation for a social relational lack, as a defense against a social structuring absence at the center of school life, is not the whole story of how individual identities are socially produced. But, it is that part of the story we see enacted as high school youths struggle to become somebody. What we see is how much identity is created as a defensive compensation to a failure in modern social relations, how the compensatory defensive processes operate as self-formative, and hints or 'foreshadowings' of a postmodern succession to modern social relations are already altering the terms of how society affects the self.

A more expansive view is that these school or class differences represent a divided identity labor, which when recomposed, offer a portrait of the *fin-de-siecle* self, or, more precisely, an institutional prologue to a vaunted postmodern transformation of self. Seen separately, there are self processes particular to each school/class: class psychology. Seen as a whole, there is an internally differentiated field upon which some historically new, postmodern or otherwise, sort of identity is created: historical psychology. Each school/class represents an aspect of the self, just as each lack — interaction, society, self — is an aspect of social relations.

The emptying of social relations induces a set of defensive self processes as compensation to the lack. The absence of reciprocal interaction in the working class school eventuates in a series of divisions or 'splits' that protects against a vulnerability created by an absence of caring interaction and completed identification with adult authority. 'Rads' and 'jocks', 'good kids and losers', disciplinary and therapeutic locales, exaggerations of male and female, are some of the divisions that occur in the absence of a consistent positive identification with a listening, though powerful adult.

In its organizational separation, between bureaucratic discipline and therapeutic understanding, Grummitt mimics the stereotypical sex role divisions of the patriarchal nuclear family. But, the organizational apparatus fails (while the family has not successfully yet completed) positive engagement with students. Teachers' own professional insecurities and career trajectories, community demands for a restoration of order and control, fiscal retrenchment, and a newer difference between students and their teachers aided by advancing mass culture and intensified economic need, all combine to dissipate the interactional trust that might produce caring identification necessary for reciprocal interaction.

This failure provokes a search for alternate routes to validate identity. On the surface it means 'hard shields' against vulnerability that comes from a lack of adult assurance and approval; leathers and wood spikes are the icons. Beyond that, it means accepting even institutional negative identities, if that's all the institution can provide. As a result, attachment is to the IMAGE, an institutional reinforcement of cultural stereotypes, that functions as a primary point of self reference instead of identification with an interactional caring, adult other person. Division is the first line of defense, underlined and secured by exaggeration of differences. But the final victor is alienated identity formation in which not a self, but an image of self emerges. The mirror replaces the subject.

Distance from the self doesn't require an elaborate institutional mechanism. For the professional middle class students, alienation or self-distancing is part of the self. It is not the apparatus, which is seen as powerless and irrelevant from the start (unlike the working class students who invest hope that the school will care, despite repeated demonstration to the contrary), which is rejecting. Instead, through a combination of ironic humor and depression, limitless performance expectations (which are themselves integral to student identity) are put under control by dampening commitment to them.

Performance is at once the medium and goal of self affirmation.

But, it is also a threatening enemy of the self, because it can denigrate and reject the self when not properly pacified. Its never-ending character — college that is beyond high school, and the career demands beyond college, and social conscience and economic status beyond career — instigates strategies of dampening, depression and distance. Self defense here is less mediated by the school institution. It is built in, brought to school, imbibed early, like the Sesame Street 'they pushed on us', a psychic ancillary to socially induced precociousness.

'The idea of the school' represents a form of society that is not an antidote to an excessive emphasis on individual performance. 'School spirit', like performance pressure, can unleash limitless expectations for commitment. Students can be committed to the United Nations club, or math team, or band. Those are delimited commitments that can be scheduled, but also contained in commitment of self as well as time. The school as a whole, society, has become 'nothing'. On the surface, students are too busy achieving to have the energy to see themselves proudly as part of something larger than grade instrumental or leisure interest activities. Beyond that, however, it is the character rather than the logistics of performance that diminishes collective capacities for society.

Socially created performance pressures carry along with them built in defenses against limitlessness itself. Society, both the progenitor and antithesis of individual achievement performance, is really united with that performance. Both are means of self affirmation, but also threats to the self. They are channels of boundarylessness, uncontrollable demand, unpredictability, and finally, self surrender. The success ethic at Penbroke requires ability to engage limitlessness, but in a controlled way. 'Mellowing out' or getting 'psyched down' is a means of self defense against performance.

'Apathy', is the students' way of describing compensatory defense against limitless demand which is represented by BOTH performance and society. Performance can be individualized, and regulated by depression. Society is compartmentalized ('departmentalized' for teachers), avoided and denied. Negation of society is part of the compensatory defense against limitless demand and the threat of an unbounded self represented by performance. It is practically more difficult to withdraw from school performance 'pressures'. Society, however, can be denied; an evaporated nothing, a haunting absence for which 'apathy' is simply a condensed label. Society becomes nothing as a method of self defense.

At the same time, there is a longing for the absent society. Students crowd 'The Public', a small designated space free of instrumental rationality. They lobby 'the administration' (a term signifying Penbroke students' depersonalization of authority, and hence, its lesser immediate relevance in identity work) to keep the Public open longer, just as 'the intellectuals' lobby for more space to put out their words in a magazine they call *The Universe*. They hang out in nearby stores, sometimes longer than they should, and like all American teenagers, they seek each other out in partying and cars.

The teachers most starkly reveal efforts to compensate for the missing social totality. They are convinced that lack of 'communication' is the school's biggest problem. On top of all their meetings, and the everyday reassertion of 'let's talk' to resolve differences, they see at least some future hope from communication experts, group process facilitators, and a so-called Japanese-style of management through communicative consensus. At Penbroke, depression is a method of self-defense and rationalized communication is a way out of social fragmentation and an absent social center. Social 'apathy', even though society seems missed, still operates to keep performance 'on track'.

Social institutions, even by their lacks, shape the self. There is, however, a difference between the interactional and society lack in working class and professional middle class schools and a more basic lack of self affirmation in the urban, poor, minority or so-called 'underclass' school. The self does not shape itself in response to a lack, absence, or emptying of some aspect of social relations. It means that the defensive process of self construction, to the extent that it is compensatory, operates at a more basic level. Self-establishment has to be repeatedly accomplished before any other direction or shaping takes place. The compensatory process is more direct. Where the lack of self affirmation is the basic social absence, the socially patterned defensive self formation occurs at the first, basic line of self defense: self existence.

If the school underlines the unrealized emotional dependency that simultaneously inhibits and makes desirable reciprocal interaction, and if it amplifies the loud silence, the effectivity, of commitment to a collective life beyond instrumental interest, how much more so does any single sign, no less social pattern, make prominent the tenuousness of the self in the urban underclass school. The classroom where a large banner in front of the room is a condensed visual representation of this point. It reads: 'I AM somebody'. The 'am' is underlined.

From the first hello that says, 'we are not who you have heard we are', to the last goodbye's pleading to remind the world that 'we have value as human beings', the students work to create a visible, differentiated and reputable self. The moral language of being 'good' or 'decent' is the way that the social comes to be represented in de-marginalizing self existence. Whatever they may have to prove about their self value at the outset of their school career is exaggerated by the school's organization around the assumption that what is lacking among the students is a decent, moral self. Morality here is not the neat, the clean concern of the upwardly mobile working class teacher, but, again, a more basic placing in question of the student's integrity. From the first early morning meetings of the administrative staff to the close of the school day, the students are managed, at worst as a potentially dangerous population and at best as a deficit self, to be classified, guided, or uplifted.

As I have argued, the 'attacks' on the self, from the hidden assumptions of student inferiority, to the indifference born of professional bureaucratization, to literally the hall attacks of the guards, or teachers' impatience received as insult, are part of the school's organized way of life. Even as intentions for betterment, education and uplift are encouraged, what is absent here is an automatic, unquestioned, and unquestionable type of social assumption that self is present, valid, moral or valuable.

The assumption of an extant self is part of the structure of modern social relations that includes the possibility of interaction and of commitment to society as a whole. In the immediacy of its effects, this lack, of the assumption of self, seems the most powerful. The depth of impacts of interactional and societal emptiness may be no less than that of questioned selfhood, but they come to the surface less readily. 'Drilling', the interaction game of verbal invidious self distinction and fighting, which is almost always a self defense against imputed moral inferiority, are preeminent social forms. The lack of an affirmed, *taken for granted* valuable self as the determinative social organizational absence induces expressive displays of self remark as the most immediate and accesible compensation to school social relations' reinforcement of socially inherited stigma.

The expressive, immediate display is a displacement for the more central doubt of self value. As a student explained, socially visible success at trend dancing groups can be taken as a sign of other self potentials and thereby operates to generalize as an inflation of self-value. School administrators, and certainly some teachers understand this process, and try to nurture it by incorporating such informal social/self mechanisms into school events and programs. Popular culture programs, where students perform for each other in the auditorium that is ordinarily used for attendance and 'tardiness' detainees are complemented by additional teacher inspired themes of self-value by emphasizing for example, Black culture, heroes, and history. Some students participate in these activities, but rely for more regular self-sustenance on less socially aggregated events. Small groups of close friends, 'cuz (cousin) bones kin', even when they are sites of invidious 'drillin' for self value, provide self affirmation. Who you 'hang with' reflects appreciation to you.

The 'politics' of school, which is the politics of self affirmation against the extra-school and intra-organizational lack of self appreciation, works through the successful establishment of interlocking friendship groups. The peer network isn't just the place where you reinforce your image, or where you communicate. It is a social structure integral to self construction. Emptying taken for granted self value from the school institution induces constructing networks as the forward-looking, foreshadowing defensive maneuver against self denial.

Just as aspects of the self — emotional, performative, moral — are not exclusive to one school/class, but are instead its salient aspect, so too with the defensive processes within which students create their identity. Division and 'hard shields' are not defensive, identity-forming actions that belong only to Grummitt's 'rad' youths. Distance and a controlling depression of achievement expectations can be found outside of Penbroke's social perimeter. Expressively displaced displays of self and the immediately pressing politics of reputational selves occur among all teenagers, and not only for the morally inferiorized minority students at Washington High School.

Indeed, taken together, these defensive processes of a self formed within institutions characterized by social practices of emptying core elements of social relations are, I think, more revealing of what postmodern society means practically, than general, textualists' talk about a 'decentered', postmodern self. While our description only tells part of the story, it ties self dynamics to organized social practices in concrete everyday institutional life. Analytic recomposition of what I have presented as a class divided self, formed as a compensatory defense against a class specific institutional lack in social relations, shows, contrary to the usual postmodern view, an unwillingness to accept centrifugal self dissipation as easy herald of a new ahistorical epoch. Identity is formed in *defense* against social absences, not in welcoming acceptance.

A potentially emergent postmodern self would be a recomposition of what I have referred to as the class specific 'foreshadowings' of *image*, *communication* and *network*. This self too emerges out of social interactional labor for preserving self against social lacks and beyond the first line of more directly compensatory actions of self construction. These actions, despite evident overlap, are class specific strategies that are at once strategies of self defense and self construction. While incomplete, both theoretically and from the vantagepoint of individual biographies, these primary compensations offer a guide to differences in the class self: divided, distant and displayed.

Divided Self

Students always bring a life history to school. At Grummitt, there are important differences of family experience. There are small town children from traditional families whose lives are centered around church activity. There are children of skilled workers, for whom job security in All American City, especially working at The Company has afforded opportunity to own suburban tract houses. And there are children whose single-parenting mothers struggle for economic survival. There are differences among the school staff, in their social backgrounds and pedagogical and ideological orientations. But, school life at Grummitt covers over these differences to present the portrait of teacher insecurity and burn-out and student rejection, contained anger, and socio-emotional hunger that I have described.

Division and amplification and hardening of small differences is how everyday life is managed at this working class school. The rads are 'scum' to the jocks. But rads can do jock activities like football and jocks can do rad activity like skipping class or smoking dope. Social organization, created everyday by all the social actors at Grummitt, forms potentially fluid and small differences into fixed positions, cultural territories, and separate, encased identities. The division between Bech and Lyborg, like polar magnets at different ends of the hall, shows how the apparatus can respond differently; offering on the one hand, a clearly male, bureaucratic discipline, and on the other, a female, nurturant therapeutic understanding. Bech's province is larger and superceding as the prevailing core form of social relations between adults and youths. Lyborg's listening and helping form of relation is injected into the school from outside. That professional and culturally alternate intervention is 'retrenched', virtually eliminated as part of a wider action of state privatization that began in the early Restoration years when I was at the school and continues until now. Bech's referral system operates only because Joe Kingman, everybody's father, creates and supports the apparatus that HIS constituency, parents tired of 'liberal chaos', wants as guarantee of restored authority.

The parents may want authority and order, but the students want love and caring. Teachers efforts to meet those needs are blocked by an independent trajectory which limits their professional commitment. They too lack 'care' and professional self-realization through an autonomously motivated pedagogical interaction with their students. They adapt by dividing work and private life — family and leisure time in which they try to recoup both the giving and receiving of positive emotions that has become blocked within the school because of a conjunction of the historical structural and cultural changes. The teachers care, but increasingly outside the life of the school, and out of reach of students' expressed needs.

The discipline machine of the assistant principal's office is the most formal, rational instance of students' experiences of rejection. The general silence between teacher and student about the shared and different conditions of their lives is not new for many youths, who 'take shit for whatever you do' as the loudest punctuation of familied interactional emptiness. While the school's rejection, whether at the extreme of disciplinary expulsion or simply by inhibited communication with the adult educating professionals may not be the first or deepest such wound, it hurts because there is hope that school is a respite and escape from an earlier silencing, if not humiliation by parental actions that range from family authority's silences to neglect and abandonment by parents sundered and wounded themselves in the struggle to get by in the larger economic world and workplace. For many students, school is a disappointment of socio-emotional hope.

The peer world is not a simple refuge from this disappointment. Nor is it a direct antidote for adult rejection. The peer world is mediated, by the school's apparatuses, particularly of discipline, and by the mass cultural images which are the materials that enable compensatory solidarity among such clearly oppositional groups as the rads, but among jocks and thespians as well. Mass culture provides the visual and aural language within which substitute, secondary relations can be formed in the effort to complete the failed, suppressed or incomplete interactional satisfaction with adults.

The peer world is derivative in two senses. First, it is not the creative collective cauldron for cultural alternatives that 'counter-cultures' are sometimes portrayed as. Defensive peer groups consolidate mass cultural images and appropriate them as their own with the protection of collective witnessing. Identification with the image is a precondition of peer solidarities. Second, it is derivative, at least at Grummitt High, because it is formed either under the happy aegis of extracurricular coaches, or 'on the run from the authorities', hiding in the school's alcoves, together, AFTER rejection at the hands of the official bureaucratic representations of the adult world.

While the outside is material for self definition in the presence of others, it is also full of threat, of reminders of prior failed connection to adults and their social machines. Division is important because it reduces the scope of the outside, and so makes self defense more efficient. School organization, family and mass culture all offer gendered difference as the most pervasive and safest route to divided identity. Exaggeration of sex roles is the work of shoring up and protecting a defined and delimited, though relationally eviscerated, self.

Gender is the main visible divide here, but it stands for the dividing process itself. 'Them' and 'us', rads and jocks, good kids and losers, is recreated in everyday identity labor as a way of defending identity in the absence of reciprocal communicative relation. Social splitting occurs in the absence of interaction where ongoing revision of self and other relation occurs. This negotiation, predicated on at least a modicum of trust that there is a mutual concern, allows fluidity, shifting, and internalization of the back and forth of difference as self constitutive. Without it, there are no two way streets for difference. Only cumulation, overcoding, and self-fortification of a part of partnered dialogue that gives away its work by the clue of stylization is possible. That is how the lack of interaction builds upon emotional hunger and absence of social connection to defend against the overt and implicit rejection experienced in the institutionalization of authority and an almost inadvertant interactional silence.

What is left from this self defensive work is not simply a set of rigidly divided selves, a modern alienation, but also a substitute dependence on the media rather than any partnered subjects of interaction. 'Symbolic labor of identity formation' is a limited concept because it analyzes the after-effects of identity formation under conditions of interactional absence. It is too forward looking, working interpretively beyond the construction of divided selves as compensation, and taking the derivative role of images as a natural given of social interaction. 'Symbolic economy of identity' is correct to the extent that interactional subject alienation succeeds, and supra-personal images prevail as the primary referent in the process of self construction.

The modern self, for the working class school is divided. Division is a compensatory device in the face of absent mutual interaction. Material for self construction is not created either in dyadic interaction or even defensive social aggregates. It is imported from mass culture, constituted as the image to which defending self refers itself, while gaining simplifying validity by exaggerated imaginary divisions.

What emerges, I think, beyond the divided character of this element of the modern self, is the medium of its constructive work, supplanting the original with the imitation. The image becomes a basic aspect of what may live on past the first line defense of division, a foreshadowing component of a postmodern self that emerges from an institutional absence of interaction.

Depressed Self

Professional middle class youths are, by their own acknowledgement, living in the future, rationalizing the present, feeling burdened by the weight of achievement expectations, and calming down in order to regulate the pressure of escalating and invidious performance demands. Not all students at Penbroke are children of the professional middle class, and not all students experience the burden of high performance expectations from their friends and families or cope with that burden by 'staying calm', or bursting out with self-expression by writing on the wall, or trying to violently erase all such public communication.

There is an expectant atmosphere of academic excellence and rosey futures, where prestige college admission is the first step. Students will tell you, first thing in the day, how harrassed, how 'behind' they are in their assignments, or how poorly they did on the last test or how they're so unprepared that they'll likely flunk the next one. Much of this sort of talk is psychic bet hedging, self dampening that preserves the pleasure of success when one does not only not fail the next test, but gets an A or A-grade. Talk that downplays achievement also assures the competition, your friends, that you have not completely succumbed to your parents' performance control, that you are a normal, all around person with other things to do and problems to solve beyond perfect preparation for grade success. This shared self dampening of achieve-ment expectation is a method for containing competition sufficiently to enable the maintenance of friendships, in which you can find some commiseration, but also focus on diverting matters like clothes, boys or girls, cars and music.

At the top of the class, peer self dampening pays off. You really do have pleasant surprises of success, and you can continue harboring the ambition that you will enter the chosen circle of acceptance at the best colleges. When it doesn't happen, and although the college acceptance rate is very high, not everybody gets their first golden choice, then we hear the adaptation that I described among intellectual seniors' reflections on what they might have missed in school life and how they do the difficult work of 'getting psyched down' (An odd expression, since most of the time, I hear students at Penbroke 'getting psyched UP', or its equivalent, simply 'getting psyched'.)

Typically, the normal student tries hard, but learns not only to at least expressly dampen expectation in order to limit competition so that a normal identity and the friends that go with it can be maintained, but amplifies and generalizes the dampening of performance expectation. 'Staying calm', or 'mellowing out' becomes a generalized method of self regulation. Along with the control of a continuous bombardment of expectations to achieve from all quarters, other 'ups' and 'downs' come under the modulating effort. Students do, of course, still 'get psyched', but there is an awareness of the self defensive value not only of not expecting too much, but also of feeling too much. Where identity worth is closely tied to achievement, the process of deflation becomes a generalizable strategy of self defense.

Emotional self-regulation, especially of 'ups', which, if not realized, carry a dangerous weight of self blame, internal stigma and guilt, fits well with the conscious attention to a rationalized self regulation of all activity. 'Flex' scheduling represents educators' attempts to break the customary bureaucratic hold of set classroom lesson times. What happens at Penbroke though, is that the responsibility for social co-ordination in the school is at least in part transferred from the bureaucratic structure to the individual conscience. It is the students who obsess about time. Even the 'intellectuals' accept responsibility for the rationalization of time. Penbroke is neither the totalizing bureaucracy of the old ghetto fortress school, Washington, nor the emotional battleground that Joe Kingman presides over with force of personality at Grummitt. Here, a highly individualized collectivity takes into its separate selves a series of regulatory practices, which it codes as 'responsibility', or more precisely, 'professionalism'.

Beyond the surface press for achievement, that is the real mark of the Penbroke student: responsibility and professionalism. The juggling and rationalizing of time for well-rounded achievement closes off some activities, especially anything that is unbounded and cannot be easily predicted as to the duration or depth of commitment. How much emotion and self-expression is shut down and depressed in the course of forming a responsible, professional school self is difficult to gauge. Surely not all vandalism represents what I have called 'violence against the null totality', or outbreaks of hatred and rage against the school as a whole, as several teachers suggested. There are examples, like theft of chemistry lab scales, that are quite instrumental. Still, Janey burning posters off the school walls leaves an afterimage. Less violent forms of self inscription into the school's physical totality, like grafitti, do also stand for outbursts of self expression, of a desire to inscribe the self to the social; if not within it as enactment, then on its surface, as memory. There are vivid interruptions to a more pervasive practice of mellowing out.

'Apathy' is also a less violent expression of rejection of the school. Unlike Grummitt, apathetic withdrawal is not a defensive reaction against rejection by school authorities. At Penbroke, school authorities, abstractly rather than personally identified, not as Bech or Lyborg, but as 'the Administration', are put at psychic arms length by the students. While teachers' approval may be needed, for even something more than the necessary grade approval, it is the teachers more than the students who become objects for evaluation. Students talk less about whether teachers listen to them, respect or care for them, and more about teachers' competence — their professional performance.

Apathy is part of the depression of expectations and rationalizing process of self-regulation that enables responsible performance in salient spheres of action. In a reversal of Grummitt, it is not the school which does not care about its students, but the students who do not care about the school. Apathy is rational depression of action directed toward the collective, which complements self-dampening as message given off to peers and self, and a more profound calming that depresses feeling to protect against the disappointment of wrongly predicted 'ups'. Apathy is the depressed self's defense against the social totality of the school.

Commitment to the school, apathy's opposite, endangers a temporally organized and emotionally even and self-regulated self because it builds on the desire for responsibility and threatens to overwhelm it with limitless demand; just at the time that 'learning to manage my time' and 'mellowing out' have defended successfully against the limitless boundaries of never ending achievement expectation. Social commitment, commitment to the school over and above instrumental interest activities, makes the already depressed self vulnerable to further defensive depression if it cannot realize the responsible achievement which has become its main orientation to action.

Responsibility is a precondition of commitment, which amplifies the threat of limitlessness posed by achievement and tempered in responsibility, professionalism, time management, and the depression of feeling and expression. Commitment opens up what has already been closed in the struggle to regulate achievement and represents a heightened danger of limitless performance demand. Apathy is social depression, which at once defends the responsibly depressed self against

further demand, and deprives it of the possibility of achieving more
aggregated levels of social integration and solidarity.

Talk substitutes for solidarity. While the teachers most starkly
show how 'communication' is a response to the sense of belonging
that is lacking, both students and teachers do generally acknowledge
that something is missing in the social life of the school. The missing
'spirit' is of the totality, the collectivity, the school as a whole, the
'idea' of the school. Commitment threatens reminders of achievement's
limitless performance demands. Communication, however, can, like
time, be rationalized, planned, and, when inconvenient, readily reduced
or eliminated. Students, who are less far along the professional track
than the adult educators, do not yet have packaged communication
manuals as guides for social relations. But, like the adults, they may
connect and disconnect interactions with the marker of 'let's talk'.

The importance of communication as a substitute for commitment
and identification with the social whole may only be fully developed
later in the life course of the professional middle class. For the youths
though, talk is less demanding than commitment and they, perhaps
more than the adults, recognize that in matters of social commitment,
they may be more talk than action. In classrooms, there is an interest
and concern with 'social issues'. There is an international awareness,
replete with innovative travel and interchange arrangments abroad.
But, the student who wondered whether her schedule would permit
her to do anything about a nuclear holocaust was ironically presenting
other students' doubts about the distance between interests in social
issues, which many of their parents espouse, and social commitment as
a form of action. They know that all the space, and more, of desire
that cannot be easily limited has already been occupied by individual
performance. Any further limitless demand would activate equilibrating
depressive defenses, and while students don't ordinarily articulate such
connections, they do know that they don't want to become any more
depressed. Social commitment, under these conditions, is not something
to 'get psyched' about. Communication may be a foreshadowing defense
against the absence of society, and a precursor of a postmodern self
built on the emptiness of society itself.

Displayed Self

The absence of a taken for granted affirmation of self in the urban
'underclass' represented at Washington shapes student response to
the school's regime. School control and surveillance reinforces student

suspicion that school shares wider social denigrations of their value. Even helpfully intended teaching is interpreted as intentional embarassment and demeaning of students by teachers. How much more so is the classification system, which the school needs to obtain additional state funds, perceived as an unjust devaluation. Most of all, monitoring the public space with coordinated surveillance and punishing violators, within a regime of perceived diminution of tolerance, in an organizational gradation of bureaucratic-legal discipline, underlines an assumption of a self under attack by the official world of successful, largely non-minority adults.

Tough talking, cutting classes, or, on the other side, keeping the struggle to become somebody through academic achievement and 'proving' oneself in the eyes of the school's adults are all responses to the fundamental perceived devaluation of the self. Crichlow (1991) refers to 'those who try and those who won't'.

The most pervasive response to self devaluation occurs in the identity work students accomplish in their peer social lives. This peer life is not a simple mirror image haven from rejection or compensatory caring as it is at Grummitt, or a leisure relaxation and diversion from the boundless pressure to succeed that it is at Penbroke. Interaction with peers is the alternative ground for affirming not a particular direction or orientation for self realization. It is instead, the place where basic self existence is validated.

The compensatory defense against self devaluation is a revaluation process that, because of the depth and pervasiveness of the devaluation, has to be immediately, urgently and continually reaccomplished. That is why 'drillin', informal, though rhetorically elegant verbal put downs of others is such an important every-day skill. And that is why fighting is so prevalent. As I have described, fighting is almost always self defensive. Its prevalence testifies to the extent and volatility of self sensitivity. 'Don't mess with me' should really have a second clause that reads, 'because I have been messed with so much and so systematically by so many people and their social apparatuses that what is left is very raw, and worn right on my sleeve'.

Reestablishment of the attacked self occurs often outside of school, by which I mean not only in the immediate locale, which it does, but also, back in the student's own neighborhood. 'Street life' is an alternative to the work of trying to make it in school. Making it in school is explicitly about academic achievement that gets you over the system to graduation, the army, a good job, or even to college. But, 'making it' in school is less openly, but more extensively, about establishing a sense of self worth *within* institutions like Washington that are from a time and still, at least to some extent, from an adult staff that represent other worlds. In street life, the logic of drillin' is materialized to 'hustlin', where oneupmanship is realized beyond verbal display in economic establishment through marginal activities like pimping, gambling, or more serious 'criminal' action. 'Hustlin' is about making it on the outside, without the legitimacy of official institutions like Washington. While it is more about getting around than over the system, ultimately it is about the same goal of having a decent and valuable self to display to others so that they may confirm to you what you continue to doubt: 'you are somebody'.

Reputation is everything, and school interaction is understood, by at least some students, as more than an academic path. Its immediacy is in the politics of the self, using the expressive capacities of informal networks to offer indisputable displays of self value. Visibility has to be heightened in proportion to the degree of self doubt. More than for Grummitt students, images are not objects of identification, but rather resources to appropriate and stylize into and on the self in ways that insure its remarkability. It is not identification with an alien image, but its display in order to call attention to the differentiated existence of its bearer that typifies this relation to a wider mass culture. That is why dancing or skating may be as, if not more, important than clothing. Attention-drawing from peers is intensified, without the working class' expectation of its provision by teachers and their consequent disappointed, internalized rejection.

The displayed self is a defensive response to the lack of taken for granted self affirmation and to prejudices and social practices of moral inferiorization. It is the 'whole attitude' of the students that is questionable to the school's staff. School, for most Washington students, does not overcome the prejudice of moral inferiority, but reinforces self sensitivity, forcing short run self protective assertion.

The depth of moral questioning prompts immediate, visible display and continuous self establishment. You have to prove it now — decency, competency, even adulthood, which for girls often occurs by the seemingly short route of pregancy and parenting. You want to show your value and have it recognized on the spot. You can whip out your credit card, wear some noticeable uniform of value, or produce your child. High achievers, following The Company role models, are less captive to the status politics of reputation and display; but at Washington they are what Crichlow (1991) calls the 'minority subculture of achievement'. For the others, you come to school to meet your friends and to overcome a generalized perception of devaluation, which the school then unintentionally reinforces by its attempts to insure bureaucratic conformity.

Reputability can be picked up on the go, by anonymous subtle acknowledgments that you are not someone to be messed with, or by clever repartee, drillin', with casual acquaintances. Networks provide more predictable sources of status recognition for visible displays of proven self value. The deeper the wound and the more tenuous self definition, the more it is necessary to make self points in each inter-action and the more important it is to infuse the interaction with selfness.

Displayed performance, in dance, but also in dress which can glean ongoing responses of recognition, is the main compensatory defense to social relations where the existence and basic moral value of the self is placed into question. Networks are the infrastructure of reputation. They foreshadow the social mechanism of self-production where more long term, stable institutional processes do not operate to create a taken for granted self, but instead, either by their explicit message or by virtue of their fragility, self has to be continuously re-affirmed. Self-establishing interactional practices come to occupy more and more of the entire space of social relations.

In these conditions, politics of relationship or of totality give way to the politics of the self. If a postmodern self is ephemeral and dif-fuse, its signs dissipated outward to fiberlike networks, then these high school youths are a vanguard, offering a foretaste of the future. The self is negotiated quickly, by its outward signs. Stability depends not on some form of inwardness, but on a capacity, now called politics, to activate multiple responses to signs along recognizing networks.

Recomposition

Each 'class self' may be considered as an element in a combined con-figuration. While there are overlaps and combinations of 'selves' across schools/classes, the 'ideal types' have been presented here to emphasize class differences and to show how different self processes can be described as responses to specific determinative absences in social relations within class institutions.

These differences in compensatory, defensive selves can, however, be thought of together, as one inclusive, historical self. There is a coexistence of defenses. Division, denial and compartmentalization can operate alongside depression and intense self control, while even the displaying self of the devalued ego can be imagined to fit such an historical type. Indeed, the simultaneous impact of gendered, class and racial division within contemporary 'advanced' society implies that the identity infrastructure of these social forms also functions simultaneously. While continuing social class division lends credence to emphasizing the differences, we are able to see how emotional, performative, and moral orientations are combined in a composite self. Similarly, we can imagine the defensively formed self responses to lacks in modern social relations, as a composite.

This composite is the 'modern self'. At once: hungry for emotional dependence, desparate for a caring responsive other; but also obsessed with limitless demands for individual performance, missing commitment to something larger, though unable to accept its potentially boundaryless demands; and, in its weakened phase, requiring and questing ongoing self assurance by expressive display, cultivating verbal and visual arts of invidious differentiation. There are, of course, innumerable efforts to describe and analyze such a self (see, for example, Wexler, 1983; Lasch, 1984).

The point here is to see the formation of self much more closely in relation to specific social practices within institutions, and especially to underline the degree to which lacks in social relations are different and determinative across class institutions. In this view, the modern self is formed during a time of institutional emptying, or even, from the vantagepoint of modern understandings of social relations, of institutional failure. It is a defensive self, split in emphases along class lines, that when considered in totality represents an array of strategies, all of which protect the emotional, performative and moral needs and interests of a self, which, however tenuous, contained or divided, seems to emanate from a unified center.

The 'second-line' of defense, responses emerging from the same set of social lacks, that I have called 'foreshadowings', can also be seen less in their school/class related differences and more as a composite. Image in the working class, communication in the professional middle class setting, and network at the urban 'underclass' school all emerged from students' interactional self defensive work. Division, depression and display are the primary types of defense. Secondary, less developed aspects of student identity formation emerge to suggest possibilities of a new composite self in formation. Out of institutional emptying, and beyond the direct construction of defensive selves, this new composite suggests what is being created that looks beyond current lacks in social relations.

This composite approximates a 'postmodern self'. Here too, while there are more discursive fantasies than we might like about such a social self type (Wexler, 1990), the point is to trace the emergence of the elements from specific institutional practices, including emptying and absence. Whether these particular secondary defenses will develop, move from a defensive to a more intiatory direction, and combine to form such a composite postmodern self, will, I think, be better answered by further empirical study of social insitutions than by allegories of textual deconstruction and decentering in the social and individual body.

Significantly, current discourse about an epochal shift in the self is virtually silent about any continuing class differences. The ideal composite occupies the whole stage of speculation, despite its deracination from describable changes in the organization of social life. I have insisted before (Wexler, 1987) that poststructuralism should not be readily separated from postindustrialism. Likewise, talk of a postmodern self belongs in the context of particular historical changes in macrosocial organization and microsocial, everyday institutional practices rather than as an aesthetic extrapolation from postmodern textualism.

Here, there is only a beginning made to think of any emergent 'new' self in historical, social and institutional terms. While I believe that the so-called 'education crisis' is the leading edge of the wider crisis, studies of self in socially different schools will, I hope, be complemented by further study in other institutional spheres. Or, perhaps, without interaction, society and self, such empirical study will itself appear irrelevant, a discursive form belonging to the iron, industrial age and its culture and theories that will have all disappeared.

Chapter 7

Horizon

Academicism

New sociology of education that began as a political articulation, ended in consumption of alien, popular academic discourses. Postmodernism was at once the flashiest, but also the most academicist of these status displaying academic languages. What was lost along the way was not only historically meaningful political commitment, but also the interest and capacity for social analysis.

As a writer of new sociology and postmodern texts, I think that they are valuable and illuminating discourses. But, in abstraction from historical social and political movements and from everyday social institutional lives, the discourses degenerate to rhetorics, and then, like all overused language in 'advanced society', into consumer slogans, which circulate in the university in the form of academicism.

I have tried to use postmodern insights, not as a display, but in order to help make sense of social life. Reciprocally, lack and absence I take as institutional processes, which may be borrowed from philosophical and literary analyses, but which are meaningful to the social analyst because, in very unpostmodern terms, they are grounded in everyday social life. While the discourse may be illuminating, I think it is also engaging because it amplifies and represents ongoing, organized social events. Without that grounding, all such discourses operate as tools of alienation, and render the theorist in sociology and education a latecoming status seeker to the acdemicist university forms that were ruled for a decadent moment in industrial capitalism's cultural history by literati. Like large segments of the professional middle class to which they belong, they have generally eschewed commitment to society, and have ignored class society.

The postindustrial, and therefore, the postmodern moment, is not over. But, the iron culture of industrialism is not quite finished either. 'American revival in manufacturing' headlines the *New York Times* (February 5, 1991). 'Fears of de-industrialization were overblown', said Robert Lawrence, an economist at the Brookings Institution (page 1). Gazing toward postmodernism wrongly led new sociologists to abandon analytically an infrastructure that was not abandoned in practice. New sociologists of education left off studying institutions, especially the workplace, that had earlier been seen as determinative. Yet, there is now some recent work, such as that of Catherine Casey (1992), which returns new sociology to that interest by a reanalysis of the postmodern workplace in relation to self and education.

There are many paths out of academicism. My emphasis here has been on interpretive empirical study of social relations and the self in the context of school institutions that I see as exemplifying and representing wider differences in social class life. The drive to this analysis is not cumulative encyclopedism, to make sure that nothing is left out, to have all the analytical pieces. Rather, the analysis is driven by an historical politics in which identity has become a lynchpin between organized institutional life and social movement. Alberoni (1984) stated it most succinctly: movement and institution. What we call 'change' (Touraine, 1989, of course is the most longstanding critic and explicator of how the concept of change inhibits understanding of social life as collective social action) is repeated transition between institutional and movement aspects of social life. He, like Durkheim, Freud, Marx, Weber, Pareto and Buber, understood also the centrality of self transformation for and within historical institutions and movements.

Perhaps because new sociology became truly and unintentionally an embodiment and exemplar of postmodern culture by virtue of its discursive eclecticism that ended as collage, if not pastiche, this historically central analysis of self in relation to class institutions, was not analyzed or discussed (for a somewhat less social exception, see Pinar, 1991). I hope that these snapshots of school life in All American society help turn attention to the institutional dynamics of the self, and to the importance of developing a social psychology of school, and a class psychology of institutions.

Identity Politics

The general analytical interest comes less from a need for theoretical or discursive comprehensiveness and more from the desire to understand self transformation as at once an individual life and collective, social understanding. Behind and beneath the understanding is desire to affect the course of individual and collective life. In the current moment, this is politically as well as analytically redemptive work (this section is adapted from Wexler 1991). For, even that apparently 'critical' segment of the professional middle class to which I belong has for a long time been engaged in a process of sublimation of social analysis into discourse and the sublimation of its practical dilemmas and possibilities into 'theory'. Marcuse (1964) may have believed that sublimation into high culture — in this case, theory — offers the grounds (or heights) for transcendental reflective negation. There can be (Marcuse, 1955: 154) a 'non-repressive mode of sublimation'. Art, while it may later be seen as succumbing (Marcuse, 1964; 65) to technological repressive rationality, is the liberatory Orphic and Narcissistic moment of a transcendant, 'reality'-negating, aesthetic dimension. But current social theorizing in elaborating the discourse, including high textualism, is not libertory. It is a REGRESSIVE SUBLIMATION. The professional middle class critics used theory 'fantastically' to avoid a less mediated encounter with everyday social reality. That sublimation is now institutionalized in a current accomodation of critical theory to postmodernism, poststructuralism and textualism. There is a dialectic of high culture. Negation of the socially taken for granted, the status quo, is only one side; the other is avoidance and escape into elaborately sublimated fantasies as theory, discourse and text.

While the institutionalization of the regressive sublimation as theory now continues in the surplus production of discourse, there are historical conditions that lead to a DESUBLIMATION of the encounters with social reality that were formerly avoided. One effect of such desublimation will surely be increase in the repressive desublimation that Marcuse described: a 'controlled desublimation' that is 'nowhere (society's) negation'. Instead of a mediated culture of critique, there is a release and absorption of libidinal energies into commodities and the administered total society.

The question that I raise is whether there is a critical moment to desublimation in which the process of theory and discourse as avoidance that characterized an earlier moment is now reversed. In such circumstances, a less mediated relation between self and society would lead to renewed interest in social analysis rather than discourse and to an investment in practically transformative activity rather than theory. This possiblity, of a PROGRESSIVE DESUBLIMATION is a narrow path, fraught with the danger that it really signals the end of critical reflection on society. The bet, however, is only by getting out of the discursive fantasy can the direct object of social life ever again be critically appropriated.

The current desublimation, which importantly includes a re-engagement of libidinal energies in performance or reality principle activities rather than transformation of energies into 'culture', artistic or transcendental reflection among critics in the professional middle class is the result of several simultaneous processes. First, there is in postmodern culture a new 'end of ideology'. Now, not affluence or consensus obviates the need for critical grand theories. Rather, the willing incorporation of transcendental, autonomous (Habermas, 1981) cultural realms into mundane social life and the inversion of critical distance into participatory parody makes superfluous the need for a theoretical 'outside', or archimedes point. In the same postmodern vein, the diffraction of a unified subject diminishes desire for a subjective origin to any critical gaze, no less systematic articulation. Postmodernism (Lyotard, 1984) hails the passing of the 'grand narratives' as the earlier epigones of cultural/theoretical desublimation applauded the 'end of ideology'. Paralogy, after all, is a principle of performance, however local or randomized.

Within this larger shift, cohort histories of producers and consumers help create the turn away from discourse and theory to analysis and practice that I am calling a potentially progressive desublimation. The professional middle class carriers of the rationalized, academicized ideologies of the youth movement are now middle-aged. Foss and Larkin (1986) in their analysis of postmovement phenomena write: '. . . the psychic consequences of a social movement become denatured in the forms of psychic healing and upward mobility of former members of dissident collectivities . . . movement sensibilities are effaced by the necessity to return to the production of the material necessities of existence' (p. 137). Or '. . . society moves from periods of quiescence to movement, with a transitional phase following the movement, whereby former movement participants are forced to accomodate themselves to the recrudescence of dominant structures. Dissidence during the postmovement period is fragmented, ritualized, and isolated' (p. 138).

At the same time, there is no mass local economy of critical ideology consumers. From an historical, movement analysis, the socially structured forms of domination and oppression during the transitional period are not yet collectively articulated into a new ideal definition of reality. Accomodation and assimilation pervade consciousness, while changing forms of domination make earlier movement world-views into irrelevant ideologies. 'The next Left', Foss and Larkin observed (1986; 158), '. . . will laugh at us'. Meanwhile, the sluggish local market for critical theory is bolstered by the globalization of the economy and an attendant importation of 'offshore' students. Likewise, discursively elaborated critical theories are exported and circulated in the ideologically fertile Pacific rim countries.

Marcuse's discussion of 'repressive desublimation' (1955; 1964) in the one-dimensional society makes clear how freed energies are directly incorporated into a commodity system that blocks their use for liberation. Sexualization of society is accomplished at the cost of eroticism, and the satisfactions achieved by lifting of complete instinctual repression are 'controlled satisfaction'. It is an 'adjusted desublimation' that fuels a 'happy consciousness' of the advanced capitalist form of totalitarianism. Such a desublimation, like contemporary 'busyness' is a practical and effective ideology.

The dangers of the current desublimation, whose development I ascribe to postmodernism's version of end of ideology by death of the grand narratives, postmovement accomodation, and prematurity of the 'next Left' among youth, go beyond repressive desublimation by sexualization for commodity cathexis. The flattening out of transcendence also occurs by excessive absorption in the performance or reality principle. Repressive desublimation is a characteristic of production as well as consumption. The release from theoretical avoidance and escapism does not have a straight path to social analysis and transformative practice. The first stop of practicality is instrumentalism and the routinization of engagement with the real world that is internalized as obsession. If fetishism is the defense of the consumptive sphere, mediated by commodities, then obsessive and ritual thought and action is the defense of the productive sphere. The apparatus of bureaucratic rationality does not crumble before the inquiring mind. Rather, inquiry is first channeled, tamed to the immediacy (unmediated) of 'problem-solving' within questions generated by the criterion of smooth-functioning.

Both types of repressive desublimation — the fetishism of commodities and the obsessive instrumentalism of performance — block the emergence of critical, reflexive, transcendental possibilities. What is especially dangerous about the present, is not simply the successful elaboration of commodity fetishism into mass neurotic addiction (Slater, 1980) or the dissolution of the self into a spectacular nodal mirror trying to catch glimmers of recognition as Langmann (1990) so vividly describes. The 'deeper dynamic' (postmodernism forbids the imagery of levels or depth), is the simultaneity or *combination* of the repressive desbulimations or collective neuroses of BOTH consumption and production. Foss and Larkin recognize this new condition (1986: 146) as the 'generalization of repressive desublimation' on the one side, and on the other, an 'apparatus of social discipline' that is based on 'scarcity-stimulation'. *Both* commodified instinctual substitution satisfaction and 'surviving' in the corporate production apparatus by ritualized adaption and problem solving act to inhibit the successful passing through of desublimated energy into critical social analysis of production and consumption and of the development of a collectively enacted, subjective authentic organization of transformative practical action. This is no longer a question of 'discursive blockages' to historically appropriate forms of critical theory but of the internalization of *social character* — fetishism, addiction, obsession — that inhibits the subjective realignments (Alberoni, 1984) which are the prerequisite to a 'nascent state'; the moment or rebirth that precedes historical collective, transformative actions.

Characterological blockages, and especially the contradictory relation between them, sets the stage for the next historical round of social movement. By movement, I follow Alberoni (1984) as well as Foss and Larkin (1986) for whom a social movement is revolutionary. Foss and Larkin distinguish social movments from protest or 'episodic dissidence (1986: 132): 'So long as these three aspects of a social movement are a mutually reinforcing totality — intensification of conflict, reinterpretation of social reality, and redefinition of the self and its capacities — a social movement is ongoing'. For Alberoni (1984), the 'nascent state', the transition to a new social order, represents a failure of existing forms of social solidarity and a 'consciousness' in which 'what appears to be' is contingent and incomplete (p. 58). 'The nascent state': '. . . corresponds to an abrupt alteration of the preceding order of social solidarity and to the birth of a new solidarity' (p. 84). The break with everyday, institutional life and the failure of solidarity is necessarily accompanied by a change in the self, or as Alberoni puts it a 'restructuring of the subject's field of experience' (p. 95). A social movement is defined by a revolutionary moment in which the old institutional order fails to work either in social solidarity or in self definition, investment and experience. The 'next great shift' as Ehrenreich (1989) puts it, for the professional middle class, will require not only a 'shift in consciousness', but an attendant subjective or self transformation that is not ideological or fantastic (p. 257). Rather, it will build on the historical structural conditions that set the collective terms of self-definition, realignment, and transformation.

The primary social basis of a movement that works through the process of self transformation is the contradiction between the subjective demands of consumption and production. I think that the initial youth movement of the professional middle class, like historical movements generally (Alberoni, 1984; Foss and Larkin, 1986), required the sense of a new and other world, that included a radical reorganization of the self or ego. A new movement is possible that is created from contradictory socially structured, subjectively experienced demands experienced as *ambivalence.*

Social contradictions are the precondition for the sort of ego ambivalence that Alberoni describes as the core of the 'nascent state'. (1984; 84: 125). Ambivalence of love and violence that is normatively controlled under conditions of everyday institutional life, reaches a threshold where attachments, cathexes, social relations or investments require a reorganization to reduce ambivalence to tolerable levels. The moment of reorganization or subjective realignment, the nascent state, is where '. . . one, eros, violently seizing new objects in its grasp, and the other destroying the structures that imprison the former and investing the old love objects. Compared to the obsessive constraint that preceded it, the experience is one of liberation' (p. 102). There is 'an economy of eros and violence' in which intensified ambivalence is the trigger for a collective, socially shared and communicated self transformation. Durkheim's 'collective effervescence' is the theoretical precursor to the nascent state.

Ambivalence or internal conflict can be contained by patterned methods of ego defense. Cultural mediation of the self/society relation now performs that function. Ashley's (1991), Langman's (1991), Luke's (1991) and others' (Slater, 1980; Schneider, 1975) analyses describe postmodern forms of commodity fetishism. How the socially patterned defenses that contain ambivalence work from the mass culture to the organizational level (Labier, 1986; Hirschhorn, 1988) still requires a good deal more description. The collective/self relation is mediated by culturally reinforced and represented obsession and compulsion as well as fetishism and addiction. The study of collective neurosis that postmodernism and its critics describe corresponds to typical self dynamics in the consumption relation. The 'spectacular self' is television's self (Kroker and Cook, 1987). Self limitation and neurosis is, however, also created for the 'working wounded' (Labier, 1989) in the postindustrial workplace (Hirshhorn, 1988). Postmodernism sublimates necessity and performance as well as sexual desire. Yet, its representation, even critically, is of the culture of consumption.

The career is no less powerful a determinant of the life-world among the professional middle class than is its free-time commodified fetishism of visual imagination. While the self is spectacular or even imploded, it is simultaneously over-instrumentalized. If self-reflection is absorbed in pervasive media image and sound, practical action is rationalized into increasingly informationalized decision nodes. What Noble (1991) describes in the genesis of the 'man-machine symbiosis' paradigm in military/educational research is the end point of a more self-invested and self-mediated process of worklife. The consumer self is diffused while the producer self is condensed. One is attached to its object fetishistically, while the other is tied by disembodied performance obsession.

The contradiction is socially structured, between production and consumption, and subjectively experienced, between the happily dissolute and seriously retentive self. The intense press toward self-reorganization will occur when the now protected boundaries of the institutionally split self give way to integrative forces. The press for integration is economic; rationalization for a more efficient subjectivity. Ultimately, the quest for greater performance and productivity, under the intermediate guise of healthfulness, demands an end to defensive ego-wastefulness. There is a way out of the iron cage: rationalization destroys the internal defenses that help reproduce it. The new movement is a deformed, revised holism, one that will have to redevelop self and social integration from the residues of the historic contradiction of an agonized class.

Education

Beyond, and more practically eventful than the academic discourses of new sociology of education and postmodernism, there is a contemporary public debate about the importance of education for society. There is a a great deal of talk about an 'education crisis'.

The current crisis in education is posed as an economic one. The prevailing theme has been that America will lose its global economic advantage if it does not educate its youth for the technological capacities that are required for the new information age of electronic production. The thesis is simply that without more success on a wider scale within education, there will be an insufficient level of human resources necessary for economic competition; therefore, education must be reformed.

There are so-called 'social' analyses of the crisis in education, which argue not only that education has an important impact on the economy, but that the social origins of students have an important impact on their educability. Poverty leads to deficits that impede schooling for a well educated work-force.

Of course education is important for its influence on human resources and for economic development and, of course, poverty affects the education and human development of a growing segment of the American population. But, the crisis in education is more than one of relation between the school and the production system or the family.

The crisis of education is a crisis in the school itself, and that crisis is a crisis of society. Education is the leading edge of a broader institutional problem that links all our institutions, including economic, family, religious and political. The education crisis is first and foremost a crisis of *public life* in the United States. The school is a crucial site of public, social life, and a crisis in the school is a sign of a broader fundamental social problem.

While there is not quite as much rhetoric as with the education/ economy relation, or in the discussion of educational reform, there is also some discussion about the decline of public life and threats to democracy. What I have tried to do is describe specific processes by which one can see inside the school what is usually talked about only in general terms.

The main thing about schools is that they are one of the few *public* spaces in which people are engaged with each other in the interactional work of making *meaning*. These are places for making the CORE meaning, of self or identity among young people.

In their own words, students are trying to 'become somebody'. They want to be somebody, a real and presentable self, anchored in the verifying eyes of friends whom they come to school to meet. While they are aware of a life after education, in the occupational world of work, and in varying degrees acknowledge interest and attention to the learning of school subjects, their central and defining activity in school is to establish at least the image of an identity. 'Becoming somebody' is action in the public sphere, and this is what life in high school is about.

The crisis of education takes different forms in the high schools attended by children of different segments of society. There is no one decline of the public sphere. There are distinct processes of an unintended, but patterned withdrawal of people's energies from organized public life. That is what is happening in these schools.

Cognitive research has been the academy's corresponding contribution to the economically important 'education crisis'. Douglas Noble (1991) has traced the institutional history of current emphases on work-related cognitive skills and educational technology, underlining both the military influence on current cognitive thought in education and the redefinition of these human cognitive skills as only the 'human factor' in complex machine systems. He critiques this transformation of education from an interest in human understanding to efficient human factor performance in cybernetic systems.

The portrait of schools in *all* American society is part of the same effort to argue for the importance of the 'non-cognitive' elements in education. What matters most to the youths I studied is their struggle to become somebody, to establish their identity through social relations. What we found was how much the absence or lack of core elements of modern social relations shaped the youths' struggles. Educators, like new sociologists, have concentrated on cognitive skills, curric-ulum or 'knowledge', to the neglect of identity. The portraits in this study are a corrective to that neglect, but still leave unanswered a larger set of questions that would prompt research from the relation between both interests: knowledge and identity. Along with a social psychology of education and a class psychology of institutions, I see explication and study of the knowledge/identity relation as part of the horizon for future work in what we still call sociology of education.

Prognostication

What we see in these schools is not simply a crisis of educational technique, or a need for better synchronization between the school and the workplace; it is a problem in the institutional core of the public sphere, an erosion of the institutional mechanisms and processes that build social commitment. What is required is to rebuild the institutional core.

Historically, intellectuals played this role, articulating and creating beliefs which became the basis for social commitment. The culture of the emergent symbolic economy — an economy of electronic networks and numerically controlled machine production, an economy of robotics — does not yet have an ethic that creates institutional commitment.

University intellectuals are not by and large working on such an ethic and on recreating the moral bases of institutions and public life. They are themselves caught in the dynamics of a decline of public life, as it is acted out in the university. We in education are seriously engaged in a number of collaborations and connections between the university and the schools, and I expect to see more. But the sort of collaboration that is finally needed to solve the educational crisis, is for intellectual work in the university to help create a new institutional public sphere.

As long as university intellectuals remain caught in a logic of professionalism that erodes society and cannot step beyond it toward creating a new inner worldly or public ethic, then we may be doomed to live out of Weber's (1958) prophecy of modern society: 'Specialists without spirit, sensualists without heart; this nullity imagines that it has attained a level of civilization never before achieved'.

The creation of a new public sphere will require a transformation of the mission and character of the university. When that begins, we will at least be on the road to a lasting solution of the 'education crisis'.

In the transformation of the university, a shift that will be pressed by the fiscal crisis and the demographic reduction facing universities, I look toward significant alterations in the organization of knowledge. The anti-academicist press for public engagement and practical meaning for scholarship and science, which is of course vulnerable to an incorporative anti-intellectualism, may, I think, also lead to internal university reorganizations of knowledge that challenge traditional subdivisions of the disciplinary university. Combined public press for socially meaningful knowledge and university reorganizations may in time lead to revolutions in knowledge equivalent in scope to the scientific revolution. Simultaneously, the symbolic economy of numerically controlled machines and robotics and a displacement of social relations by networked communication of images may push knowledge past public interest and disciplinary dissolutions and reconstructions toward programs of cybernetic maintenance of wholly new social actors.

At the dawn of the bureaucratic industrial world, Weber queried who will inhabit such a society. My own sense is that despite strongly emergent elements of an equally great shift toward a new social world, we will live for some time within decadent institutions, which in part survive by holding out the promise of progress toward a postindustrial or postmodern world, while perpetuating the present. 'Foreshadowings', despite some basis in social reality, belong to an over-arching psychic regime of primary collective compensations and methods of self defense. Only when those defenses are surrendered will we see what industrial capitalism really was and what may be possible in the future. But the surrender of defenses will require a level of selflessness that we now do everything in our power to prevent, because we identify it with death.

The reclamation of self required to mobilize transformative institutional movements out of the present will occur, sooner or later, through rigidification or dissolution, on the path of institutionally weak, but tenacious reproduction of defensive selves. Whether by breakage or surrender, a new self will arise in the midst of defensive and anticipatory social forms. 'There is more day to dawn', Thoreau (1960) wrote, 'The sun is but a morning star'. And Whitman (1965) sang:

Out of the dimness opposite equals advance, always substance and increase, always sex,
Always a knit of identity, always distinction, always a breed of life.

Chapter 8

No Note on Method

The convention in this genre of work is to have a methodological appendix in which one reflects on the work one has done. Instead of that, I have tried to start out with that perspective even from the beginning, in talking about this work as a work of composition and by working back and forth, and sifting out from within the analytic description. In a sense, the first chapter constitutes the 'traditional' methodological appendix. My point is that the reflection is a somewhat distanced moment, but is not an addendum to the work itself, but an integral component in its creation.

Still, I have indulged in the pleasure of ironic self reflection about doing field research in social science. In chapter 4 of *Social Analysis of Education*, 1987, I built on Bill Livant's paper, 'Working at watching' (1982) to spoof the pretensions of my critical colleagues who saw ethnography as a method of transcendental distance — and therefore of analytical privilege. As we saw in the analysis of methods of self defense, more narrowly instrumental 'research' methods can also be used as qualifiers and modes of distance from even an inessential substance of commitment.

I certainly appreciate the seriously coded promise of playfulness contained by field workers' reflections on their methods — which has itself become a profitable postmodern sector within the academic culture industry. We have already reached the point at which such reflections displace the work itself to a protective cultural regime of postmodernism, that I have argued also has an institutional basis. Instead of replicating and legitimating that regime, our work, I think, is to analyze it in the hope of doing better, not only theoretically, but also practically.

We shall need to go beyond postmodernism, not only in cultural theory, but also in institutional practice. A contribution that social analysts can make is to do good closeup empirical work and to try to make sense of what they have seen. If we are looking, as I am, toward a new social world, then there is only so much time that can be allowed on the playful ground of methodological reflections, deconstructions, and evasions. The challenge, in research as in practice, is to put one's shoulder to the wheel and do the work that is necessary to help create this new world. It does not require a new realism to make the constructive and reflective moment integral to the work itself.

As I indicated, members of the research team pressed me for a more action-oriented research approach. While I applaud the emergence of action research, and expect that in education there will be a great deal more of so called 'collaborative research' between the participants and the 'analyst', I worry that between deconstructions and reflections on the one side, and action-oriented research on the other, the analytical moment that is both within and outside of the observation and dynamic practical action will be dissolved and forgotten. Within that moment or pivotal point between playful nihilism and earnest realist reformism, there is a self awareness that is at once simultaneously collective and also social and constructive. I think it is within that awareness that research can play both a critical and constructive role in going beyond reflections on the current disenchantment and decay. There have been enough deconstructions of ethnographic method. What we need now is to write ethnography from the vantagepoint of the future.

Bibliography

ALBERONI, FRANCISCO (1984) *Movement and Institution*, New York, Columbia University.

ALTHUSSER, LOUIS (1969) *For Marx*, London, Allen Lane.

ANDERSON, GARY (1989) 'Critical ethnography in education: Origin, current status and new directions', *Review of Education Research*, pp. 249–270, Fall.

APPEL, STEPHEN (1992) 'Psychoanalysis and "New" Sociology of Education: Positioning Subjects', unpublished Ph.D. dissertation, New York, University of Rochester.

APPLE MICHAEL (1982) *Education and Power*, London, Routledge and Kegan Paul.

ASHLEY, DAVID (1990) 'Playing with the pieces: The fragmentation of social theory', in WEXLER, P. (Ed.) *Critical Theory Now*, London, Falmer Press.

BAUDRILLARD, JEAN (1988) *Selected Writings* (edited by Mark Poster) California, Stanford University.

BERNSTEIN, BASIL (1990) *The Structuring of Pedagogic Discourse*, London, Routledge, Kegan and Paul.

BERNSTEIN, RICHARD (1983) *Beyond Objectivism and Relativism*, University of Pennsylvania Press.

BOURDIEU, PIERRE (1984) *Distinction: A Social Critique of the Judgement of Taste*, Massachusetts, Harvard University Press.

BOWLES, SAMUEL and GINTIS, HERBERT (1976) *Schooling in Capitalist American*, New York, Sage Books.

CASEY, CATHERINE (1992) 'On what is learned at work: A study of the effects of the discursive practices of work on the self', unpublished Ph.D. dissertation, New York, University of Rochester.

CRICHLOW, WARREN (1991) 'A social analysis of black youth commitment and disaffection in an urban high school', unpublished ED.D dissertation, New York, University of Rochester.

EHRENREICH, BARBARA (1989) *Fear of Falling: The Inner Life of the Middle class*, New York, Pantheon.

161

FOSS, DANIEL and LARKIN, RALPH (1986) *Beyond Revolution: A Theory of New Social Movements*, Massachusetts, Bergan and Garvey.

GEERTZ, CLIFFORD (1980) *The Interpretation of Cultures: Selected Essays*, New York, Basic Books.

GIROUX, HENRY (1983) *Theory and Resistance in Education*, Massachusetts, Bergan and Garvey.

HABERMAS, JURGEN (1981) 'New social movements', Telos No. **49**, pp. 33–37, Fall.

HABERMAS, JURGEN (1982) *Legitimation Crisis*, Cambridge, England, Polity Press.

HABERMAS, JURGEN (1984) *The Theory of Communicative Action: Vol. 2: Reason and Rationalization in Society*, Boston, Beacon Press.

HIRSCHHORN, LARRY (1988) *The Workplace Within: Psychodynamics of Organizational Life*, Cambridge, Massachusetts, MIT Press.

HORKHEIMER, MAX and ADORNO, THEODOR (1972) *Dialectic of Enlightenment*, New York, Herder and Herder.

HORKHEIMER, MAX (1972) *Critical Theory*, New York, Herder and Herder.

KROKER, ARTHUR and COOK, DAVID (1987) *The Postmodern Scene: Excremental Culture and Hyper-aesthetics*, New York, St. Martin's Press.

LABIER, DOUGLAS (1989) *Modern Madness: The Hidden Link Between Work and Emotional Conflict*, New York, Simon and Schuster.

LANGMANN, LAUREN (1990) 'From pathos to panic: American character meets the future' in WEXLER, P. (Ed.) *Critical Theory Now*, London, Falmer Press.

LASCH, CHRISTOPHER (1984) *The Minimal Self: Psychic Survival in Troubled Times*, New York, W.W. Norton.

LESKO, NANCY (1988) *Symbolizing Society: Stories, Sites and Structure in a Catholic High School*, New York, Falmer Press.

LEVI-STRAUSS, CLAUDE (1963) *Structural Anthropology* (translated by Claire Jacobson) New York, Basic Books.

LIVANT, BILL (1982) 'Working at watching: A reply to Sut Jhally'. *Canadian Journal of Political and Social Theory*, **6**, Nos. 1–2, pp. 211–215.

LUKACS, GEORG (1971) *History and Class Consciousness*, MIT Press.

LUKE, TIMOTHY (1990) 'Touring hyper-reality: Critical theory confronts informational society' in WEXLER, P. (Ed.) *Critical Theory Now*, London, Falmer Press.

LYOTARD, JEAN-FRANCOIS (1984) *The Postmodern Condition*, Minnesota, University of Minnesota Press.

MARCUSE, HERBERT (1955) *Eros and Civilization*, Boston, Beacon Press.

MARCUSE, HERBERT (1964) *One-Dimensional Man*, London, Routledge and Kegan Paul.

NOBLE, DOUGLAS (1991) *The Classroom Arsenal: Military Research, Information Technology, and Public Education*, Falmer Press.

PINAR, WILLIAM (1991) 'Curriculum as social psychoanalysis' in KINCHELOE JOE L. and PINAR, WILLIAM F. (Ed.) *The Significance of Place*, Albany, New York, SUNY Press.

SCHNEIDER, MICHAEL (1975) *Neurosis and Civilization: A Marxist/Freudian Synthesis*, New York, Seaburn.

SLATER, PHILIP (1980) *Wealth Addiction*, New York, Nutton.

THOREAU, HENRY (1960) *On Man and Nature*, Mount Vernon, New York, Peter Pauper Press.

TOURAINE, ALAIN (1981) *The Voice and the Eye*, New York, Cambridge University Press.

TOURAINE, ALAIN (1988) *Return of the Actor*, Minnesota, University of Minnesota Press.

TURNER, BRYAN (1990) (Ed.) *Theories of Modernity and Postmodernity*, London, Sage.

WEBER, MAX (1958) *The Protestant Ethic and the Spirit of Capitalism*, New York, Scribner.

WEBER, MAX (1963) *The Sociology of Religion*, Boston, Beacon.

WEIS, LOIS (1990) *Working Class Without Work*, New York, Routledge and Kegan Paul.

WEXLER, PHILIP (1983) *Critical Social Psychology*, New York, Routledge and Kegan Paul.

WEXLER, PHILIP (1987) *Social Analysis of Education: After the New Sociology*, New York, Routledge and Kegan Paul.

WEXLER, PHILIP (1988) 'Symbolic economy of identity and denial of labor' in WEIS, L. (Ed.) *Class, Race and Gender in American Education*, New York, SUNY Albany.

WEXLER, PHILIP (1990) 'Citizenship in the 'semiotic society' in TURNER, BRYAN (Ed.) *Theories of Modernity and Postmodernity*, London, Sage.

WEXLER, PHILIP (1991) 'Afterword' in WEXLER, P. (Ed). *Critical Theory Now*, London, Falmer Press.

WILLIS, PAUL (1977) *Learning to Labour: How Working Class Kids Get Working Class Jobs*, Westmead, England, Saxon House.

WHITMAN, WALT (1965) *Leaves of Grass*, New York, NYU Press.

ZUBOFF, SHOSHANA (1988) *In the Age of the Smart Machine: The Future of Work and Power*, New York, Basic Books.

Index

Please remember that this is a library book,
and that it belongs only temporarily to each
person who uses it. Be considerate. Do
not write in this, or any, library book.